Manager's Guide to Strategy

Other titles in the Briefcase Books series include:

To learn more about titles in the Briefcase Books series go to
www.briefcasebooks.com

A
Briefcase
Book

Manager's Guide to Strategy

Roger A. Formisano

McGraw-Hill

New York Chicago San Francisco Lisbon London
Madrid Mexico City Milan New Delhi San Juan
Seoul Singapore Sydney Toronto

The **McGraw·Hill** *Companies*

2 3 4 5 6 7 8 9 0   FGR/FGR   0 9 8 7 6 5 4

ISBN 0-07-142172-6

*This is a CWL Publishing Enterprises Book, developed and produced for
McGraw-Hill by CWL Publishing Enterprises, Inc., Madison, Wisconsin,
www.cwlpub.com.*

This publication is designed to provide accurate and authoritative information in regard to the subject matter covered. It is sold with the understanding
that neither the author nor the publisher is engaged in rendering legal,
accounting, or other professional service. If legal advice or other expert
assistance is required, the services of a competent professional person
should be sought.
> *—From a Declaration of Principles jointly adopted by a Committee
> of the American Bar Association and a Committee of Publishers*

McGraw-Hill books are available at special quantity discounts to use as premiums and sales promotions, or for use in corporate training programs. For
more information, please write to the Director of Special Sales, McGraw-Hill,
2 Penn Plaza, New York, NY 10121-2298. Or contact your local bookstore.

Library of Congress Cataloging-in-Publication Data

Formisano, Roger A.
  Manager's guide to strategy / by Roger A. Formisano.
    p. cm.
Includes bibliographical references and index.
  ISBN 0-07-142172-6 (pbk.)
  1. Strategic planning. 2. Business planning. 3. Strategic
planning—United States. 4. Business planning—United States. I.
Title.
  HD30.28.F6783 2003
  658.4'012--dc22

                                                2003017209

Contents

Preface

Mention business strategy to most managers, and this conjures up images of an army of high-priced MBA consultants with fancy charts and PowerPoint presentations. Strategic planning meetings, often cloistered in far-away places, generate binders full of grand schemes and sometimes little else. At some companies, strategy is shrouded in mystery, discussed in hushed tones, and left as the exclusive domain of top management. This book is about changing these images of what strategy is, what it should be, and how strategy should be developed.

First and foremost, strategy is the way we decide to achieve our long-term objectives. Strategy answers the question "How do we best accomplish our goals?" Strategy is therefore about decisions and actions that will contribute to your business success. But where do the good, new strategic ideas come from? The answer is that good business ideas can come from anyone in the organization. Exceptional companies want all their employees to be engaged in searching for, and implementing, innovative ways to improve the business. The main purpose of this book is to provide a resource for all managers to assist them in contributing to the formulation of strategy for their companies.

Strategy development involves three principal questions:

- Where is the business today?
- Where do we want the business to go?
- How are we going to get there?

Throughout this book, you'll find concepts, tools, insights, and examples of business strategy in the making. From setting and communicating goals, evaluating current performance, exploring the business environment, knowing your customers, and creating strategic choices through implementing new ideas, the goal is to arm readers with the capability to make a difference for the better in their own organization. If you are passionate about your business, this book strives to provide to you a guide to understand and add to the strategic decision making of the company.

Many companies deal with strategy once a year at a strategic planning retreat. Truly successful companies recognize that strategy development is continuous, and iterative. Continuous because things change; interest rates move up and down, technology changes, and customers' needs vary. Strategy is iterative because competitors, suppliers, and customers act in response to our strategic decisions. So we need to anticipate these responses, or react to them. By preparing all managers to think strategically, the organization is in a much better position to sustain a successful operation.

Sports analogies are used often in business, and also in this book. One of the best images I know for business strategy in action is the sight of a University of Wisconsin varsity eight-crew boat on Lake Mendota in Madison. The power of a boat is not determined by the strength of any individual rower, but rather in the power of every oar working together in unison, committed to the leadership of the coxswain. So too in business, the more each manager works in concert with the strategic direction of the company, the more successful the company will be in reaching its goals. Furthermore, I firmly believe, and experience bears this out, that as each manager contributes to defining the strategy of the organization, the easier, and better, strategy can be implemented and communicated throughout the organization.

In the final analysis, excellent business ideas are the fuel for the long-term success of a company. By giving all managers the factors, process, and tools of strategy, we hope that they will develop, and execute, more and better business ideas to the benefit of all stakeholders.

Special Features

The idea behind the books in the Briefcase Books Series is to give you practical information written in a friendly, person-to-person style. The chapters are relatively short, deal with tactical issues, and include lots of examples. They also feature numerous sidebars designed to give you different types of specific information. Here's a description of the boxes you'll find in this book.

These boxes do just what their name implies: give you tips and tactics for using the ideas in this book to intelligently undertake strategy development and implementation.

These boxes provide warnings for where things could go wrong when you're thinking about strategy and what might work for your organization.

These boxes give you how-to and insider hints for effective strategic planning.

Every subject has some special jargon, including strategy development. These boxes provide definitions of these terms.

It's always useful to have examples that show how the principles in the book are applied. These boxes give you the specifics from a variety of companies, large and small.

This icon identifies boxes where you'll find specific procedures you can follow to take advantage of the book's advice.

How can you make sure you won't make a mistake when planning your strategy? You can't completely, but these boxes will give you practical advice on how to minimize the possibility of an error.

Acknowledgments

My strategy expertise and experience is based on working with some great managers and mentors over the years. In particular, I single out Cliff Adams, J. Finley Lee, John Schienle, Donna Shalala, Jim Reidman, George Cochran, and Len Caronia. Many thanks and appreciation to John Woods and the staff of CWL Publishing Enterprises for the opportunity and their assistance in producing this work.

Finally, I appreciate more than anything a great family: my wife, Paula and my children David and Lisa.

About the Author

Roger A. Formisano is Professor, and Director of the Center for Leadership and Applied Business at the University of Wisconsin-Madison's School of Business.

He returned to the University of Wisconsin-Madison School of Business in 2001 after nine years in the private sector. During that time, Formisano affiliated with the Chicago-based, Cochran, Caronia & Co., a full service investment bank focused upon the insurance and financial services industries.

Prior to affiliating with CC&Co., he was Executive Vice President and Chief Operating Officer of United Wisconsin Services, a multi-line, publicly traded insurance company. He founded and served as President of the subsidiary Meridian Resource Corporation.

During his first fourteen years at the University of Wisconsin-Madison, he was Professor of Risk Management and Insurance, served as Chairman of the Athletic Board from 1988-1992, and in 1989 was awarded the Steiger All-campus Distinguished Teacher Award. He has authored over 20 articles in professional and academic journals, and consulted with companies and government agencies, including: General Electric, DEMCO, Inc, Federal Trade Commission, Foremost Guaranty Corporation, and Blue Cross and Blue Shield United of Wisconsin. He currently serves as a director of Integrity Mutual Insurance

Company, the Horace Mann Mutual Funds, and the Greater Milwaukee Open PGA Tournament.

He received his BA in mathematics from the University of New Hampshire, and his Ph.D. in business from the University of North Carolina at Chapel Hill. You can contact him at rformisano@EXECED.bus.wisc.edu.

What Is Business Strategy?

P rior to the Green Bay Packers-Chicago Bears game, the Packers coach is asked about his feelings about the game.

"We have a good game plan and our players, coaches, and support staff are prepared and ready. I couldn't be more confident of victory!"

On the other side of the field, the Bears coach says virtually the same thing.

Then the game begins. Play after play, the coaches adjust their game plans to reflect the circumstances. They keep using plays that gain yardage, they keep going with defensive formations and tactics that prove effective, they exploit any weaknesses they find in the other team, they react to injuries or field conditions, they make decisions based on the score and field position and the clock.

In the end, the team whose coach best understands the strengths and weaknesses of both teams and then strategizes for all the possibilities and whose players execute the strategies best will usually win. Then, after the game, both teams must begin again to prepare for the next opponent.

The Game of Business

Business competition is very similar to sports. In business, teams of individuals face each other in competition for employees, customers, product innovations, and profits—among other goals. The major difference between sports and business is the relevant time frame. (Imagine if teams in the National Football League had to play each other every day, from nine to five, with the lunch hour replacing halftime!)

As in sports, business organizations that win consistently excel at preparation, planning, and execution. They know their situation, know where they want to go, and determine how best to go there. Maybe more importantly, these organizations have their finger on the pulse of the markets, customers, technologies, and other innovations that may change the rules of the game and the factors that lead to success. And these dominant companies are willing to adjust their game plans accordingly.

![Key Term easel icon] **Strategy** A detailed plan for achieving success, the bundle of decisions and activities that we choose to achieve our long-term goals. Strategy is the path we choose. Every organization has to figure out what it wants to achieve and then how it is going to make it happen, with its products, customers, and operations.

Strategy is the business word for game plan. All businesses have strategies, either planned or unplanned. This book explores how to find the best strategy for your business and how to use strategy to drive successful business results, that is, achieve your long-term goals.

The Power of Business

The essence of business can be depicted in a simple diagram (Figure 1-1).

This diagram suggests that a business is a flow model, a going concern. First, there's the business idea that motivates us to begin a business.

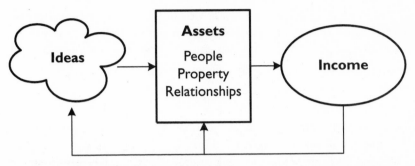

Figure 1-1. A simple model of business

Let's say we decide to use our grandmother's recipes to open a restaurant. We figure that since we all loved Grandma's cooking, others would too. In order to realize and deliver the promise of the business idea, we must use a package of assets: people, property, and relationships. We'll need a location, tables, chairs, china, silverware, and a lot of restaurant equipment and supplies. We'll need cooks, waiters and waitresses, dishwashers, and other employees. We'll need a liquor license, public health certificates, and accounts with food suppliers of meat, produce, and so forth. These assets must then generate income, which is used to refuel the assets (buy more food and pay the staff) and invest in new ideas to keep the business going. Let's examine each component of the model.

It all begins with a business idea. Now, a business idea is more than just an idea. A business idea has two defining characteristics.

First, a good business idea meets an unmet need in the market. The product or service that we offer must satisfy a customer's unmet need. This may mean a brand-new product or service or it may mean finding a way to provide a product or a service at a lower price than is currently available. In the case of our restaurant, the unmet need may be as simple as providing a good place for authentic Italian food. Certainly, there are other restaurants, and other Italian restaurants, but our idea is to package the food, wine list, and ambiance in a way that will be attractive to patrons.

Second, a good business idea drives transactions. Whatever product we offer to customers, they must be willing to exchange their money for our product or service. The test of a good business idea is whether people will give up their cash to get our products or services in enough numbers to keep operations going. Our Italian restaurant idea, when communicated to the public (by advertising and/or word of mouth), must create a demand for hungry people to select our establishment for lunch or dinner. The ultimate test is whether our business idea will meet the unmet needs of the market in a way that customers will return, again and again—and satisfy our business need to generate income.

Business Idea

There are a lot of ideas around, but they aren't all business ideas. A business idea has two defining characteristics: it meets an unmet need and it drives transactions. In a way, both can be summed up in the simple question, Do enough people want what you'd be offering enough to pay enough for it? Evaluating those three "enoughs" is crucial.

Once we have a business idea, we must assemble the assets to construct our business. Usually we need money, financial capital. Also we need employees, human capital. Finally, we need relationships: with suppliers, the government, customers, distributors, and others to make the business work. Linking the business idea with the right asset mix is what creates the power of a business and it's that link that's our business strategy. So, while we start with Grandma's recipes, in putting together our plan, we must make many decisions and undertake many activities. That is, we must construct our strategy. The location, the market we target (families, upscale diners, college students, and so forth), the décor we select, the pricing of our entrées, our wine list, the training and performance of the wait staff, the quality of the foodstuffs, and the preparation of the food—all will play a role in our success.

These *strategic* decisions we make in building our organization and business model are endless. The link between our business idea and the assets we select is our business strategy. It doesn't matter whether we are operating a small restaurant or a giant telecom, automobile, or chemical company; this coordination between the business idea and the asset mix we select is the power of our business.

The result of our idea-asset connection is the income the business generates. The lifeblood of a business is the cash flow, which is used to replenish the assets and develop new ideas to keep the business going. If an asset does not contribute to generating income, we should get rid of it! If, for example, we generally have unused tables in the dining room and yet the cocktail lounge is crowded, we should consider reconfiguring the assets: fewer dining tables, more space in the bar! Later on we will discuss how we can develop strategies based on the efficient and optimal use of our assets.

The cash flow that our business generates is the source of keeping the business going, investing in new ideas and new assets, and reaching our financial goals. We can consider revenue and income and profit: all of these terms reflect the activity of the business. But, at the end of the day, the most important consideration to the business owner is cash flow.

Cash flow The amount of money we have left over at the end of a period in our checking account, not in accounting terms, but in cash.

Revenue The total amount of money that comes into our business from sales for a particular period of time.

Income Our revenue minus the cost of the goods and/or services we have sold for the period.

Profit The difference between revenue and costs for the period. Also known as *net income*.

The Basics of Strategy

So, business strategy is our selection of ideas and assets to meet our long-term goals. Of course, we must begin with goals—What do we want to accomplish by operating this business? There are many reasons for going into business; we'll discuss the critical steps in setting goals in Chapter 2. For now, let's just think about what "strategy" means.

We can break down strategy into three components:

- Create the strategy—What should we do?
- Implement the strategy—How do we do it?
- Evaluate the strategy—How well are we doing in meeting our long-term goals?

Formulating a business strategy is a complex task even for the smallest of organizations. Furthermore, whether you're the manager of a small group in an organization or the CEO of a large company, you'll be working with strategic issues.

Creating the business strategy begins with the business idea. In the case of our Italian restaurant, our business idea is authentic Italian cooking, based upon Grandma's recipes. But as we know, the idea is not enough.

We cannot raise capital simply by presenting samples of Grandma's cooking to the loan committee down at the bank. Rather, we must present a comprehensive plan to our lenders that details the complete picture of our restaurant, so that the bank may judge whether we'll be able to acquire the assets we need and generate enough income to completely repay our debt.

We also won't be able to hire good cooks without fully explaining how our ideas for the business will provide a good place to work now and into the future. If these people cannot see a viable business in our idea, they're not likely to commit to working to prepare the foods that will turn our recipes into revenues. Also, without a good idea of what we want our restaurant to be, we won't be able to inspire our waiters and waitresses to provide the service that will make our restaurant a special experience that will delight our customers and keep attracting business.

So formulating a strategy requires us to develop a complete picture of the business in operation, even before we implement our plan. The development of this *vision* of the business requires that we address a series of questions that will lead to a successful strategy.

An Overview of Strategy Development

Since strategy is the bundle of decisions and activities that we choose to reach our long-term objectives and since we must picture our entire business before we actually start turning our ideas into business strategies, we have a lot of thinking to do. Can we structure this strategic thinking process? Yes, as a start we should address the following questions. As we do, we will begin to see our strategy emerge.

What Is Our Business Idea?

This question forces us to decide what business we are in. This is very obvious for a new business, but it can be tricky for existing businesses. Organizations act and react and sometimes find that their business idea becomes diluted or too ambiguous to describe. As a result, managers and employees lose the focus on the founding principles that made the business successful.

Wal-Mart is an example of a company that does not lose focus and is true to its business idea. For Wal-Mart the business idea is low prices, "Always!" for a galaxy of products that most people need or want. Every aspect of the Wal-Mart operation is dedicated to delivering low prices to its customers. Wal-Mart extracts cost savings in the products it stocks by being tough on suppliers and executing a sophisticated, high-technology supply chain. Corporate overhead is kept very low.

> ### Finding Our Business Idea
> **Smart Managing**
>
> The key to understanding our business idea is to understand the customers' unmet need that we're trying to address. People are looking for solutions to the problems they face; our business should attempt to solve their problems.
>
> A key point to keep in mind is that people don't buy products or services. They buy the benefits they get from the products or services. So, what benefits are we providing that meet their needs and solve their problems?

Sam's Clubs provide another low-price option through bulk purchasing and selling. Customers may not have all the brand

Wal-Mart
Wal-Mart began with the idea of solving the problems of more rural areas that were not served by large retailers and where incomes could not support high price points. Over time, as its success was proven, stores were moved into suburban and more urban areas, where Wal-Mart has met the needs of the same type of customers, those looking for one-stop shopping and very low prices for good-quality merchandise.

choices, but the selection of goods is offered at lower prices than for comparable goods sold elsewhere.

Sears, on the other hand, is a retailer that has not enjoyed the growth or financial success of Wal-Mart. If we explore the history of Sears, the company has bounced around with its own brands (Kenmore and Craftsman, for example) and with national brands. It once tried to move up-market, seeking higher-income customers, and confused its clientele with higher-price point goods. Sears has at different times been a catalog merchant and discontinued its use of the catalog. For a while, Sears emphasized "The Softer Side of Sears," seeking to promote its clothing and housewares lines and de-emphasizing the successful hardware and appliance lines. In 2002, Sears acquired Lands' End, a mail-order retailer of traditional clothing, placing some Lands' End goods in Sears stores and selling the goods through direct mail catalogs and the Internet. The casual observer of Sears might ask, "What is the business idea of the company?" There doesn't seem to be a clear answer.

If we compare the results of Sears and Wal-Mart, we find a striking comparison. Founded in 1906, Sears had revenues of $41.1 billion in 2001. Wal-Mart, started in 1969, had 2001 revenues of $193.3 billion, almost five times the Sears sales results.

Answering that basic question—What business are we in?—also leads us to consider what businesses and markets we should not be in. Sometimes it is important to say "no" to a business idea, if it does not fit our plan. We should select the best business ideas and then focus on the decisions and activities that support those ideas.

> ## Strategy Must Be Fluid
> **CAUTION!**
> The comparison of Sears and Wal-Mart should be viewed with caution. Strategy development is continuous and iterative. That means we can't stay with a failing strategy; we must try and adapt to changing markets and competition. As its markets changed, Sears should have made adjustments; however, Sears lost focus on its core business and core markets. The comparison of Sears and Wal-Mart points out the value of knowing and following a good business idea and building strategies and practices to support that idea.

What Is Our Business Purpose?

Philosophers often address the question, why do we exist? Answers usually lead to religious or secular *big picture* notions. Businesses need practical answers to the question, why do we exist? The answer is our long-term objectives.

Clearly, every business has *financial* objectives, because every business is based upon a capital investment, which should produce an expected rate of return to the owners. Yet, businesses typically aspire to be more than just an engine for returns to shareholders. Customer satisfaction, contributions to the community, and a good place to work for employees are frequently important components of long-term objectives.

Some firms provide a broader notion of their business purpose as a guide to their strategy development. Here's how Ben & Jerry's Ice Cream, for example, expresses its purpose: "Ben & Jerry's is founded on and dedicated to a sustainable corporate concept of linked prosperity. Our mission consists of three inter-related parts." It then defines its product mission, economic mission, and social mission. Its product mission is "To make, distribute & sell the finest quality all natural ice cream & euphoric concoctions with a continued commitment to incorporating wholesome, natural ingredients and promoting business practices that respect the Earth and the Environment." Its economic mission is "To operate the Company on a sustainable financial basis of profitable growth, increasing value for our stakeholders & expanding opportunities for development and career growth for our employees." Finally, its social mission is "To operate the company in a way that actively recognizes the central role that business plays in society by initiating innovative ways to improve the quality of life locally, nationally & internationally."

Other companies have a broad, but simple business purpose. Merck, the large pharmaceutical company, lists among its company values "Our business is preserving and improving human life." The American Red Cross states that it "will provide relief to victims of disasters and help people prevent, prepare for, and respond to emergencies." For the BMW Group, "The BMW brand means ground-breaking innovations and fascinating design."

The business purpose should guide the decisions and activities of the organization to create a consistent, successful, and meaningful reality. In order to achieve successful results, businesses must communicate why it's important that they exist and what it is that they stand for.

What Is Our Advantage?

Most businesses must compete with others in trying to meet unmet consumer needs. In order to be successful at attracting customers and keeping them, our business must have an advantage over the others. In the case of our new Italian restaurant, we believe that Grandma's recipes for authentic Italian food will be the advantage we have over other, more generic Italian restaurants in our area. If our advantage is meaningful for consumers, it should differentiate us from the others and lead to a successful business.

Differentiation of our product, service, or business model highlights our competitive advantage. 7 UP, the soft drink, for years differentiated itself from the soft drink leaders through its campaign, "The Un-Cola." Since 1960, Avis Rent A Car System has been proclaiming, "We try harder" to provide superior customer service, because it was Number 2. In the same industry, Enterprise Rent-A-Car has succeeded by targeting car rentals away from airports (as loaners during car repair, for example)

Your Advantage Must Be Important to the Customer

Smart Managing

In honing our advantage, it's critical to understand what drives customer behavior. We may think that real, authentic Italian cooking is important to people dining in Italian restaurants, but other factors may be more important. For instance, convenient access and parking, a safe neighborhood location, speed of service, and price may each be more important than the authenticity of the recipes and will overpower our advantage. Patrons may be willing to sacrifice some flavor for one of these other factors.

It pays to understand the nature of the customers you're trying to reach by doing some market research. For a good demonstration of this principle applied to starting an Italian restaurant, I recommend seeing the movie *Big Night*, which is the story of two brothers who open an Italian restaurant. One brother is focused on the authenticity of the cuisine, while the other brother is concerned with customer satisfaction. It's an entertaining and instructive look at defining the business.

with its line, "Pick Enterprise. We'll pick you up."

Your advantage must target unmet needs of customers. These examples suggest that companies can look to areas in which other companies fail to completely satisfy an important customer need and then create a business idea to satisfy that need and make it their advantage. Of course, if such an approach is successful, competitors will respond and copy the advantage, leading to a new cycle of innovation in the product or service that is being offered. This is what makes a market economy great. Through the competition of firms, consumers benefit by getting better and better products and services. Innovation is rewarded. Progress is ensured.

Who Are Our Customers?

If we attempt to satisfy an unmet need, we must know who has that need, since all customers are not the same. Gillette and Norelco compete for men who shave. Gillette meets the needs of those who use cream and a razor; Norelco targets those who prefer an electric shaver. Neither company focuses on men with beards (though Norelco has a product for those customers called

Market segmentation
The task of dividing the total market into groups that share common properties. Many products have multiplied to recognize various market segments and preferences.

the "Personal Groomer Beard Trimmer"). This simple case describes the need that all businesses have for market segmentation.

Few businesses try to serve the entire market for their product or service. And even if they do, they usually find ways to structure the organization to serve each market segment. In the automobile industry, General Motors tries to cover the entire market, but its division into Chevrolet, Pontiac, Oldsmobile, Buick, Cadillac, and Saturn attempts to match operating units with different market segments. (However, in 2004, GM is dropping the Oldsmobile brand. Its products are not differentiated enough in the current market for this division to survive.)

Splitting Jeans
Do you remember when there was only one style of blue jeans? Today there's a proliferation—stonewashed, baggy-fit, low-rise, boot-cut, and original Levis, among others. Each of these products is offered to appeal to a segment of the pants-buying public.

As we develop our plan for strategy, we must consider for which market segments our business idea is viable, so the idea will drive transactions. Pricing considerations are a dominant factor in market segment analysis.

Going back to our Italian restaurant idea, if Grandma's recipes require that we charge $24 for a plate of spaghetti to break even, regardless of how good it might taste, few patrons would be willing to pay that much for spaghetti and our business idea would fail to drive the necessary transactions to sustain the business.

With the wide availability of travel services on the Internet, travel agents have had to adjust from serving a broad segment to a narrow one. As travel agents had their commissions cut to zero by the airlines, they now charge clients a service fee ($15-

General Motors Adds and Drops Brands

GM led the way in understanding the various segments of the car buying public. When Henry Ford would only sell black cars, GM came out with colors and its branding strategy. Over time, though, tastes and segments change. GM added the Saturn brand to introduce a car to compete with imports, attract female buyers, and change the buying process through the no-hassle pricing policy. Furthermore, GM is phasing out the Oldsmobile brand, reasoning that it had lost its differentiation with Chevy and even Buick; and by eliminating the brand the firm could save costs and not lose customers. Similarly, DaimlerChrysler dropped the Plymouth brand after the 2001 model year, ending 73 years of production, as it was no longer worth it to differentiate between Plymouth and Dodge.

$30 per ticket) for reserving and issuing airline tickets. Since customers can go online and get tickets from the airlines directly or from providers like Travelocity or Orbitz, without paying a service fee, travel agents must segment the market and sell to those who are not willing or able to use the computer to secure airline tickets. As a result of these significant changes, the market for travel agent services has shrunk considerably. The contemporary travel agent must identify only those clients who are willing to pay extra for their services, rather than those who are willing and able to go online and serve themselves.

Market segmentation is a key component in building a successful strategy. In order to do segmentation, significant market and customer understanding and analysis are necessary.

What Is Our Product?

Our product is the benefits that we deliver to our customers. In the classic and popular TV show *Cheers*, the location was a tavern, but this bar delivered more than just drinks and pub food. As the theme song said, "Sometimes you want to go where everybody knows your name, and they're always glad you came." In a way, Starbucks has borrowed the *Cheers* model in building its business.

Starbucks is in the coffee business, but its stores deliver the same benefits as the *Cheers* bar: a comfortable place to get good coffee and share it with the same people regularly, read the paper, or just chat with friends. The product is a bundle of benefits surrounding a relatively expensive (compared with McDonald's) cup of coffee. Starbucks sells the experience as much as the coffee. And the experience rationalizes the higher price.

When customers buy a product or a service, they go through six phases:

- purchase
- delivery
- use
- supplements
- maintenance
- disposal

Purchase involves recognition of needs, searching for alternatives, deciding, and buying. If the product is not consumed immediately at purchase (like a pint of beer) or carried away (like groceries), the customer must consider *delivery* options. Some products are easy to *use*; for others training or experience is necessary. Many products require *supplements* to make them work. As products are used, sometimes *maintenance* and repair can be a concern. Finally, if anything remains of a product after use, the question of *disposal* may arise.

In the process of developing our product strategy, we must not only consider the benefits delivered to the users to meet their unmet needs. We might also consider which of the six areas of the product use cycle we are also going to serve. Here are some examples.

While most furniture stores either provide delivery or sub-contract it to a third party, Ikea, the Swedish furniture giant, does not. Ikea sells knockdown furniture that is disassembled into smaller packages that the buyer can take directly and then assemble at home. Home Depot, as another example, rents pickup trucks on-site for customers to take large items or quantities of supplies to their location.

Volkswagen initiated the bundling of service with the car and included all routine maintenance (oil changes and the like) with the sale of a new car. Other manufacturers have since followed this practice. Indeed, the parts and service departments at all automobile dealerships are there to supply supplements and maintenance. In many case, these departments bring in more money than car sales. Car dealers also provide disposal of cars, through taking them in as trades on the purchase of new cars.

Many computer vendors offer and sell training classes, so customers can use hardware and software efficiently. Camera stores sell instruction on photography and film development (and now digital enhancement) so that customers can use cameras better and realize more benefits from them and from the vendors.

Deciding on our product is more complex than first meets the eye. On the other hand, this product complexity can lead innovative companies to new and successful strategies.

How Do We Reach the Market?

The heart of any business idea is in completing the transaction. That's when the customer receives your product or service in exchange for money. The environment in which that transaction occurs is called the *distribution channel*.

One significant strategic decision we must make is the choice of distribution channel. Channels vary in their operation, cost, and effectiveness to reach particular market segments. For retail products and services, business-to-consumer (B2C), channels include the following:

Distribution channel
The way in which we reach our customers to deliver our product or service.

- company-owned retail stores
- franchised retail stores
- department stores

- direct mail
- the Internet

In business-to-business (B2B) circumstances, channels include the following:

- manufacturer representatives
- direct sales
- the Internet

Let's look at these various channels for computer sales.

Before Hewlett-Packard and Compaq merged in 2002, the companies competed in outlets like Best Buy, CompUSA, and Circuit City. For HP and Compaq, the channel of choice was department (big box) stores. Neither company owned any stores. The retail stores would order computers, stock them in inventory, and then deliver them to customers. That was the environment for transactions.

Michael Dell founded Dell Computer in 1984 with a different distribution model. Dell decided that there was significant advantage in building the computers to order, eliminating the retail stores altogether, and relying on a direct-to-consumer sales approach, using telephone and Internet channels. Customers would call Dell, design the features that they needed and wanted in a computer, pay, and then receive delivery at their doorstep a few days later. The Dell model has shown to have many strengths and has made Dell the 800-pound gorilla of the computer business. By going directly to the customer, Dell eliminated the costs of the retailer. More importantly, by building the computers to order, Dell kept its inventory of parts low;

Insurance

If we sell automobile insurance, we might do so through any of several distribution channels. We might use an independent agent, like Fireman's Fund. We might use our network of exclusive agents, like State Farm Insurance. We might use direct mail, like GEICO. Finally, we might choose to go directly to the consumer, through telephone or Internet sales, like Progressive or GEICO.

since computer component prices usually fall over time, a better cost structure was created. But Dell also received the customers' money in advance of delivering the machine, so the
cash cycle for the company was positive. The customers also
explicitly paid for delivery through a third party, such as UPS.
Finally, because of low inventories, Dell got the newest technologies to the market before HP and Compaq, which had
older-technology computers sitting in inventory.

In summary, Dell created a new business model for computer sales by switching from the traditional distribution channel. Dell offered customers a custom computer with the latest
technology at a very competitive price. It also created a lower
cost structure and a better cash flow. As a result, Dell achieved
the dominant position in the industry. Then, of course, Gateway
copied the Dell model, but it added distribution through its own
stores. Both Compaq and HP began direct sales channels, in
addition to the big box stores. Finally, IBM withdrew from the
retail store channel and now relies on direct sales.

The point of all this is that *strategically* Dell figured out how
to add more value for customers, not just by lowering prices,
but also by using technology to go the customer directly and
eliminating costs from the old way of doing business.

Another significant example of channel management has
occurred in the travel business. As little as five years ago, travel
agents sold virtually all of the airline tickets in the market.
Travel agents—independent manufacturers' representatives—
would shop all of the airlines' reservation systems and meet the
customers' requirements for schedule, price, and/or class of
service. The airlines paid the agents a commission based upon
the price of the ticket, usually 10%. The travelers never saw the
fee paid to the agent as a cost to them.

Things changed as the airlines grew their frequent flyer programs. More and more customers wanted a specific airline,
rather than other features, so that they would earn points toward
free travel. As the airline brands, through their frequent flyer
programs, grew stronger; the airlines realized that they could

Take a Look at eBay

One of the true bright spots of the dotcom world is eBay, an online auction site for almost any kind of product. eBay provides the technological platform and the "rules of the game" to facilitate transactions between buyer and seller, who may be located anywhere in the world.

Go to www.ebay.com and look around. Think about all the reasons why you might not use this site—and then see how eBay overcomes these barriers. A big barrier in Web business is trust, so eBay provides seller ratings. Another barrier is not being able to see the product, so pictures and three-dimensional videos abound on the site. Explore the wide variety and quality of products offered. See how companies are using Ebay as a channel alternative. You may be looking at the channel of choice for the future!

sell directly, without travel agents. Over time, the airlines capped commissions, then cut them to 5%, and ultimately eliminated them entirely. These changes forced travel agents to charge an explicit fee for their services. Additionally, Internet options, like Orbitz (created by the major airlines), permit customers to replicate what travel agents can do, but without paying the fee. Rather, the customer pays by spending the time making the reservation and by bearing the risk of errors.

As with computer sales, the travel example demonstrates major changes in the way in which business is done, solely by changing the channel of distribution. Clearly, the Internet creates new distribution opportunities in many markets. And new strategies will continue to emerge as technologies evolve and offer new possibilities for selling channels. The current trend is toward using multiple distribution channels rather than just one. Multiple channels complicate operations, but may provide better results.

What Trends and New Factors Will Change Our Business?

Have you ever noticed how many manufactured products that you use are marked "made in China"? Did you know that over 80% of college students do all their financial transactions on the Internet or through ATMs? What percentage of cars on the road are SUVs? Are you aware that 45% of the U.S. adult population is invested in the stock market directly or through 401(k) and similar plans? Did you know that the difference between 9% and 6% for a 30-year mortgage for $150,000 is over $300 per month? Are you aware that experts predict a serious shortage of nurses in the U.S. over the next five years?

Here's the point. The world, markets, populations, tastes, technology, and economic factors are changing—as they always have. And to sustain a successful business, we must know what the changes will be and how they may affect our business and then adjust our strategy. Sometimes changing events or factors really do not affect our business. So it's important to know and understand the things that drive success in our markets.

Wayne Gretzky, the greatest hockey player of all time, was famous for saying, "Some people skate to the puck. I skate to where the puck is going to be." Likewise, in developing our business strategy we must consider where the various changing trends— economic, legal, demographic, competitive, and social—will lead and anticipate both the trends and the business policies we must adopt.

> **Interest Rates Drive the Housing Market**
> When interest rates drop, as they have in the recent few years, one major impact is on the housing markets. Homes become more affordable as rates lower the monthly payments. As a result, demand increases and more houses sell. Those sales increase the sales of appliances, swimming pools, title insurance, and furniture, among other things. If we are in a home-related business (Home Depot, Thomasville Furniture, etc.), a key driver of our business is the level and trend in interest rates, so we watch and understand factors influencing those rates very carefully.

How Shall We Do Business?

In this context, "how" is used in two ways.

First, how do we do business from a business operation point of view? Are we cost- and efficiency-oriented? Are we

Boomers—The Biggest Trend

The post-World War II "baby boom" has been the biggest trend factor in the U.S. economy since the 1950s. This giant explosion of population has driven much of the demand for goods and services as the Baby Boomers have aged. Now those in the leading edge of the boom, born in the late 1940s, are in their mid-50s. What trends should we look for?

First, this is the age when health care expenditures for individuals really increase; expect to see significant increases in the use of medical services and drugs. Second, Boomers are thinking about retirement, so one might expect a sharp increase in the demand for second homes in the Sun Belt. Third, as Boomers retire, a higher demand for income from investments may change the demand for stocks versus bonds and other income-generating assets. Regardless of your business, it's best to know how the passage of the Baby Boomers affects the demand for your products or services and the alternatives in the marketplace.

sales- and growth-oriented? Are we customer-focused? Are we financially driven? Are our employees our most important asset? It's a matter of priorities. Call it our philosophy of doing business or call it our operational strategy. Two companies in the same industry can have the same objectives, but try to get there in two very different ways.

For a small business example, take two insurance agencies. One is managed very tightly; the owner is very frugal, drives a Toyota, and brown bags his lunch every day. The other agency is run by an owner who is very extravagant, drives a Lexus, and eats at the club every lunch. They compete in the same markets, but operate in very different ways. It's a matter of *priorities*. By operating in these different ways, the owners are defining a part of their strategy. For example, if a buyer is looking for a discounted price, which happens in all markets, the frugal operator has bigger margins and may be willing to give up profit for growth, while the extravagant owner has much less room to move and may be unable to lower the price and must, therefore, forego the sale. If the trend in the industry required more discounting in the future, the extravagant owner would be at a big disadvantage.

The second way to view the question "How shall we do business?" is our style of doing business. Are we aggressive competitors? Or are we willing to ally with our competitors? What image do we want to project? In this case, it's a matter of *values*.

Businesses have morals, personalities, habits, and images, just like the humans who operate them. In fact, businesses usually acquire the traits of the leaders who started them or who lead them to be successful. General Electric bears the distinct markings of Jack Welch, but still seeks the inventiveness of its founder, Thomas Edison. Microsoft reflects the hard-driving characteristics of Bill Gates. Enron took on the values of its leadership.

Every business can choose how it will do its business. For example, an organization can establish a zero-tolerance rule for integrity. With the recent spate of ethical problems with companies like Enron, Tyco, WorldCom, Merrill Lynch, and Aldelphia, a more careful eye is being cast toward the values that a company espouses and lives. The regulators of publicly traded companies (SEC and the stock exchanges) are adopting new rules for protecting investors and the integrity of the capital markets. Even within these guidelines, however, each firm can choose its own set of values as a matter of strategy.

A Word About Strategy Implementation and Evaluation

Developing a strategy is one thing, putting it in action is quite another. Studies have shown pretty consistently that the three biggest barriers to strategic success are these:

- A failure to communicate the strategy clearly throughout the organization
- Inconsistency between management talk and management action
- A lack of top management support for strategic initiatives

Something your dad probably told you years ago sums it up: "Say what you mean and mean what you say." Easier said than done, though!

Implementing a strategy requires leadership and attention to detail as strategic ideas flow through the entire organization and become real. Wal-Mart's strategy of being the low-cost retailer touches every aspect of the company, including executive pay, office locations, and other components of overhead.

Evaluating our strategy is a matter of management and measurement systems. In order to judge whether we're reaching our long-term objectives, we must measure our results. If we want high customer satisfaction, we must honestly measure customer attitudes toward our products and/or processes. If we want to be number one or two in every product market, we must accurately measure our market share and that of our competitors.

The purpose of this book is to provide managers at every level the knowledge, skills, experiences, and tools so their business strategies can be more effective. Whether in designing, implementing, or evaluating and modifying strategies, every member of the organization plays a significant part. Just as every player on the Green Bay Packers and the Chicago Bears must know the game plan and execute his role according to that plan, in business every manager can contribute to the execution of a successful strategy.

Manager's Checklist for Chapter 1

❑ Businesses consist of ideas and assets that generate income. The power of a business is derived from the quality of the ideas and the asset mix used to execute the idea.

❑ Strategy is the decisions and actions we take to achieve our long-term goals.

❑ Strategy development involves the process of evaluating our business situation and envisioning the future.

❑ In order to develop a successful strategy, we consider all aspects of our business—the competition, our advantage, our customers, our suppliers, our business model, our values, and the external environment.

❏ Strategy is not fixed but fluid. Strategic management is continuous and iterative.

❏ Your strategy has the best chance to be successful if it's communicated clearly and your decisions and actions are consistent with your objectives.

Goal Setting: The First Step in Strategy

Lewis Carroll, author of *Alice in Wonderland,* is famous for the following interchange between Alice and the Cheshire Cat in that whimsical book:

> "Cheshire Puss," she began, rather timidly, as she did not at all know whether it would like the name: however, it only grinned a little wider. "Come, it's pleased so far," thought Alice, and she went on. "Would you tell me, please, which way I ought to go from here?"
>
> "That depends a good deal on where you want to get to," said the Cat.
>
> "I don't much care where—," said Alice.
>
> "Then it doesn't matter which way you go," said the Cat.
>
> "—so long as I get somewhere," Alice added as an explanation.
>
> "Oh, you're sure to do that," said the Cat, "if you only walk long enough."

If you don't know where you want to go, then it doesn't matter which way you go. The lesson for *Alice* is also true in designing a business strategy. In order to plan an approach to being successful, you must define success! So strategy begins with a goal, a target for the long haul. In this chapter we explore corporate goal setting and its role in strategy development.

Corporate Goals

Read any financial or business textbook and you will find that the objective of a business is to *maximize the value of the firm to the shareholders*. Like trickle-down economics, this approach suggests that if companies create value for the shareholders, every constituency (employees, customers, regulators, etc.) will be happy. Based upon Adam Smith's famous *invisible hand* concept, maximizing shareholder wealth is said to benefit all of the stakeholders associated with the business. Of course, once again the time factor comes into play. The shareholder value creation system works if value is maximized in the long term. But what is the long term?

Most companies make financial decisions, particularly investment decisions, using the value maximizing standard. The discounted net present value method of evaluating investment options, using discounted cash flows, is clearly the best example.

Strategic Time

Time is a critical factor in making business decisions. We create a vision of the company some 20 years out. Our strategic plans usually consider a three- to five-year time horizon. Almost every company has operating plans for the current year. And publicly traded companies often make important decisions for the next quarter.

In strategy, we must match our time frame to the markets we serve and to the rate of change in those markets. Kmart, Enron and Arthur Andersen each faced important *strategic* decisions that would play out in months, rather than years. For these companies, the Rolling Stones were wrong: time is not always on our side.

> **Key Term**
>
> **Discounted cash flows** The preferred method for evaluating investment decisions. This analytical tool compares the present value of the investment amount to the present value of the future cash flows from the investment discounted at a risk-adjusted rate of return. In theory, and in many managers' eyes, the net present value—the difference between investment and discounted cash flows—represents the increase in value of the company from making the investment.

Yet, most businesses need more than that and more explicit goal-setting language to develop an overall business strategy. Strategic objectives that define what businesses we will operate, how we will conduct business, and in which markets we will compete usually are detailed. Furthermore, companies now are very conscious about the values that they stand for in conducting their activities—particularly after disclosures about companies like Enron, WorldCom, Aldelphia, and others. Finally, management often thinks about special issues like how the company treats employees and customers, its attitude toward the environment, and concerns for social responsibility issues like diversity, community involvement, and charitable giving.

So ask a corporation where it is going and you will likely hear about some clear, long-term objectives. But you will also be told of a package of ideals regarding other factors:

- The company's purpose in being
- Specific issues
- Constituencies
- The values of importance that, taken together, project a "vision" of the company in the future

"The Vision Thing"

President George Bush said in 1987 that he didn't believe in "the vision thing." His son, President George W. Bush, having faced 9/11, a slowing economy, and the war on terrorism, expressed just the opposite opinion and said that creating a vision for the future for the United States was critical for success in policy development.

Business people exhibit the same ambivalence about creating a corporate vision. Much of the negative perception about mission/vision statements revolves around the reality that for many organizations vision statements remain

> **Vision** A package of ideals and beliefs regarding the organization's purpose and values that project an image of what the business will be in the future. An organization's vision truly attempts to project a picture of the company 20 or so years out into the future.

just that: statements, some words on a page. But successful organizations make their concept of the future of the organization real, by testing every decision against the achievement of the vision goals and creating an environment in which strategy is more clearly understood and implemented throughout the organization. In recent studies, firms with formalized, articulated visions earned twice the return on equity as those firms without documented approaches. Such studies imply that there can be real shareholder value in creating a structured vision.

What does a company's vision look like? Take Starbucks, the coffee house on every corner. Let's look at what this successful company says about itself.

First, it has an overriding objective: "To establish Starbucks as the most recognized and respected brand in the world." A very lofty and bold goal! And it explains why Starbucks stores are everywhere. Notice that the company wants to achieve both brand recognition and respect, globally. So Starbucks wants to be known, but importantly it wants to be known for a certain set of operating principles that leads to respect. Interbrand, a global branding consulting company, in its 2002 survey to find the global "Brand of the Year," found that Starbucks finished in fourth place, behind Google.com, Apple Computer, and Coca-Cola. It looks like Starbucks is well on its way to achieving its goal! Its strategy is working.

Starbucks vision does not end with its objective, however. The "picture" of the Starbucks organization is clarified by its mission statement and guiding principles:

Mission: Establish Starbucks as the premier purveyor of the finest coffee in the world while maintaining our uncompromising principles while we grow.

Principles:

1. Provide a great work environment and treat each other with respect and dignity.
2. Embrace diversity as an essential component in the way we do business.
3. Apply the highest standards of excellence to the purchasing, roasting, and fresh delivery of our coffee.
4. Develop enthusiastically satisfied customers all of the time.
5. Contribute positively to our communities and our environment.
6. Recognize that profitability is essential to our future success.

The goal, mission, and principles or values provide a clear blueprint for the direction and operation of the company. While there's still room for a variety of strategies within the Starbucks operation, some elements of its strategy become very clear simply through the understanding of the company's vision. Rapid expansion of its retail operations, for example, is a nat-

Smart Managing

Look at Starbucks

Write down the Starbucks vision and then visit a couple of Starbucks stores. Stay a little while and look around. Can you see the vision in action? Do you see diversity, a commitment to customer satisfaction, and community involvement? Make notes on each of the components of the vision package and observe what elements of the strategy become apparent. For example, what happens if a customer's order is prepared incorrectly or takes longer than it should? Is it consistent between stores?

After your visits, ask yourself what Starbucks management might be doing to implement the strategy to achieve the corporate vision. Try to put yourself in their shoes: it will give you good ideas for implementing your own strategy.

Don't Cling to Your Mission

What happens if your mission no longer works? You change it.

That's what Microsoft did in 2002, as a computer on every desk and in every home was no longer as ambitious a mission as it was some 25 years earlier. So here's the new one.

> To reflect our role as an industry leader and to focus our efforts on the opportunities ahead, we have embraced a new corporate mission: to enable people and businesses throughout the world to realize their full potential.

That mission may seem very general in scope, but it's focused through the vision statement, which remains "Empowering people through great software—any time, any place, and on any device."

ural result of these positions. Emphasis on quality, customer satisfaction, and profitability clearly will lead to operational and strategic decisions that can be seen throughout the organization.

Sometimes a company's vision can be even more concise. Bill Gates and Paul Allen founded Microsoft in 1975 with a vision of "a computer on every desk and in every home." In 1975, personal computers were a novelty; today their vision is almost reality. And of course, Microsoft is now the dominant software company in the PC world. Part of Microsoft's success is directly related to their ability to see the future and then create business ideas and assets to meet the technology demands of customers.

Constructing a Corporate Vision

In many ways, a company's vision is closely related to the business idea. If we found a business without a clear vision, where would we start to articulate this important concept? Three components are really necessary to create a powerful corporate vision.

The first component is big, long-term *goals*. Remember Starbuck's goal? Objectives truly communicate to everyone what are the most important drivers of the organization's business. By stating, for example, that we want to be "number one or number two in every market" (as GE does), we communicate that size, dominance, and market power are essential to our success. Consequently, the company will likely decide not to compete in products or markets in which the field is already crowded with strong players or possibly consider a strategy of acquiring competitors. That's an example of how strategy follows goals.

The second component of vision is defining a company's *purpose*. Many firms call this their *mission statement*. In order to communicate effectively to the capital markets, labor markets, and customers, companies must know what they are about—their core purpose.

For 3M, commonly known for Scotch® Tape and Post-it® Notes, the core purpose is innovation. "Ingenuity with a purpose to see customers succeed" tells the story of a company that's focused on solving customer problems with creativity. Ingenuity and creativity are both people skills and require significant efforts in research and development investments. With this kind of a purpose, 3M must have a strategic approach to hiring the right kinds of people and investing in research and development.

For Nike, the core purpose is clearly stated as "To bring inspiration and innovation to every athlete in the world." Further, Nike makes a point to define an athlete broadly: "If you have a body, you are an athlete."

So for Nike, like Starbucks, product excellence (innovation, brand recognition) is not enough. Nike and Starbucks want to provide more direction in the way that they conduct their business. For Starbucks this yields respect, for Nike inspiration.

The final component of vision is this notion of *values*—how the company wants to act and the principles it believes in. If you go to almost any company's home page, you will find a section dealing with Mission and Values issues, usually linked in the *About Us* section. Like the other components of the vision package, the corporate values can be concise or detailed.

> ## Three Essentials for a Vision
>
> A powerful vision requires three things:
> - *goals*—long-term objectives that will concentrate the efforts of every person in the company
> - *purpose* or *mission statement*—a compelling reason for the company to be in business
> - *values*—principles that will guide the company as it fulfills its purpose and progresses toward its goals
>
> As Burt Nanus says in his book, *Visionary Leadership: Creating a Compelling Sense of Direction for Your Organization:*
>
> Vision is where tomorrow begins, for it expresses what you and others who share the vision will be working hard to create. Since most people don't take the time to think systematically about the future, those who do—and who base their strategies and actions on their visions—have inordinate power to shape the future.

Mission Statements

There's no universal format for mission statements. Each firm must find a way to communicate its vision in its own design. Yet when we begin to think about putting our vision down in writing, it's sometimes difficult to find all the pieces.

Most firms consider six areas of their business to include in their mission statement:

- products or services
- customers
- markets
- employees
- philosophy of doing business
- achievement

As we will see, some firms incorporate all these into their vision and some select among them. Our firm should consider each and then make choices to communicate its message to the constituencies.

Products and Services

One would say it's easy to think about our purpose as an

organization in terms of the products or services that we deliver. Yet, this thought has tripped up many a successful business. How many times have we read of the failure of the railroads to think of themselves in the transportation business, rather than the rail business? If IBM had thought of itself as a typewriter company, it would have missed the whole personal computer revolution. We go back to the business model and think of our products and services not in the context of current sales and uses or of features, but rather in terms of *meeting unmet customer needs.*

We might think that Intel, the semi-conductor giant, would have as a mission to manufacture leading-edge microprocessors for computer applications. Certainly that's its main business. But no, Intel sees its mission as being "the preeminent building block supplier to the worldwide Internet economy." Note that it doesn't matter what building blocks are necessary; Intel will produce them for the world, to fuel Internet commercial activity. Intel simply wants Internet-oriented businesses to see it as the supplier of choice and the problem solver for creating and sustaining e-business infrastructure.

In building our mission, then, we must not think in terms of products and services. Rather, we must answer the question, "What is our business?" in terms of meeting customers unmet needs as they evolve in strategic time.

Customers

But which customers are we trying to serve by meeting their unmet needs? Our mission should give the firm and its constituents some indication of the profile of our target customer.

Many insurance companies use independent agents to sell their products. These agents are independent businesses and usually can offer the retail buyer of insurance the choice of a number of companies to meet their specific needs. For these insurers, then, there are really two customers. First, they have to compete with other insurance companies for the agent. Then they must service the policyholder, with claims and administra-

What's in a Name?

What happens if you decide to change your segment? That's what happened to AARP recently.

The organization that began in 1958 as the American Association of Retired Persons changed its name in 1998 to AARP and began actively targeting people as young as age 50: "dedicated to addressing the needs and interests of persons 50 and older." That's because more than half of its members were still working, because nearly a third of its members were under age 60, and because an AARP study showed that 80% of Baby Boomers said that they planned to continue working after the official retirement age.

tive activities. Many of these companies clearly state in their mission statements that *the* customer is the agent. By doing so, they clarify that the agent's needs for access to coverage, speedy underwriting, commission income, and administrative ease are the issues that will drive the company.

Other organizations also need to clarify who their customers are. Hospitals, for example, surely must care for patients, but referring physicians and doctors who use their operating rooms are also customers. Some firms need to make clear that they serve a particular segment, like women (Avon or Oxygen) or the elderly (AARP). In every case, organizations must think about their business model and the people they will and will not serve.

Markets

Where will we compete? When a firm considers its markets, it generally looks to answer this question. Are we a regional, national, North American, or global? Will we compete for commercial business only or also for government business? Are we retail or wholesale? Each of these questions comes up on a daily basis in the context of conducting our business; our articulated vision and mission should clarify for the organization how we will react.

As we saw earlier, Intel will serve the worldwide need for Internet infrastructure and components. Our Italian restaurant, on the other hand, will serve our neighborhood, town, or com-

Smart Managing

Mission Statements Are Written on Paper, Not Stone

While our core purpose and values may not change, opportunities and results, good and bad, can have a dramatic effect on our mission. Both success and failure breed opportunities to review our mission and revise it. Most companies start small, serving well-defined customers and limited markets. As their business and brand grows, they should consider opportunities to expand the original concept of the business.

munity. Yet we will have to decide whether our restaurant will get into the catering business in addition to serving customers at our location. And undoubtedly, as we succeed, we will face the issue of opening other locations.

Employees. "Our employees are our most valuable asset." A cliché? All organizations need to deliver their promise, their goods, and their services through their employees. Yet, some places are considered great to work at, while others are consistently fighting to find and keep employees. Can a mission statement make a difference? The obvious answer is found in that old adage, "Actions speak louder than words." Yet, it's precisely the words we choose in our mission that will guide our actions.

Every year in January, *Fortune* magazine features a special report, "100 Best Companies to Work For." In 2003, Edward

For Example

Expanding on Burgers and Custard

Culver's began as a family business in 1984 in Sauk City, Wisconsin. They served fast food, including the ButterBurger® and real cream custard to tourists bound for the Wisconsin River and the resorts at Wisconsin Dells. Over time, their success led to opening more company stores and later to creating franchise opportunities. The Culver family frequently revised aspects of their mission regarding the scope of their business, although they steadfastly maintained other aspects relating to cleanliness, quality, a varied menu, and the ingredients associated with their custard and burgers. Today Culver's has 200 restaurants in the upper Midwest and Texas and an active franchising business, none of which they contemplated when opening their first store.

Jones, the investment house, repeated as the number-one employer. Companies are ranked on their investment in employee training, job growth, cash and non-cash compensation, and a number of other factors related to the worker experience. Two-thirds of their score, however, is determined by an employee survey of the work life and culture of the organization. In Edward Jones's case, two important factors are that the company is employee-owned and the firm spends 3.8% of its payroll on education, which represents about 146 hours of training per employee per year.

Firms that score high on lists such as the *Fortune* report clearly are managed with employees' interests in their vision and mission. When you look at the Edward Jones story, you will see that the company explicitly states:

At Edward Jones, our employees are our most valuable investment in the future. That's why they:

- Receive attractive salaries and unique career opportunities.
- Do meaningful work that is constantly changing and evolving.
- Enjoy successful careers without sacrificing their personal lives.
- Enjoy limitless opportunities for professional growth.
- Work in an environment of professional respect.

At a company like this, the employees' welfare is not an afterthought, but a major part of the organization's strategy.

Philosophy of Doing Business. Philosophy of doing business is not esoteric. It's simply about the organization's priorities, its values, and its style in the marketplace. Philosophy can evolve from the founders or from the marketplace in which the firm competes. Philosophy can also

> **Business philosophy** A statement of the organization's priorities, its values, and its style in the marketplace. The philosophy defines the approach that a company takes in its operations and sets the general guidelines for doing business.

Key Term

emanate from the current leaders. In any event, philosophy of doing business sets the tone and the attitude of the organization and its people, particularly if it is articulated clearly and acted upon regularly.

Most companies try to communicate which values are important. Some energy companies are more environmentally responsible than others. Some automobile companies are more safety conscious than others. Some companies are very active in their communities, while others are relatively silent. Some firms believe in promotion from within; others take a "hire the best" approach. Some companies punish unethical and unsavory behavior with speed and severity, yet others tolerate various levels of dalliance.

AFLAC, the insurance company with a duck spokesperson, makes no bones about its marketing style in its mission. AFLAC states its mission as "To combine aggressive strategic marketing with quality products and services at affordable prices to provide the best insurance value for consumers." AFLAC is telling the world that it is not laid-back, but rather a more in-your-face seller of insurance products. Compare AFLAC with Northwestern Mutual Life, "The Quiet Company"!

At CDW, the large computer seller in Chicago, the philosophy of doing business is very clear: "CDW's founding principles are organized into the 'Circle of Service' philosophy, where 'everything revolves around the customer.' As the framework for our business model, the Circle of Service keeps everyone at CDW focused on our customers." CDW sells over $4 billion in computers to small and medium-sized businesses and ranks 13th on the *Fortune* survey.

Without that guidance at the organizational level, a company's philosophy of doing business is left to the individuals engaged in the business activities. So, to most companies, it's important to communicate the values and behaviors that are the most important in the vision of the company. Of course, these value standards must be lived and managed consistently and regularly throughout the company for them to really acquire meaning. For example, Whole Foods Market, the organic grocer, states, "We pledge to donate at least 5% of our annual net profits to not-for-profit or educational organizations."

Achievement. By "achievement" we mean that the organization must be clear about the specific goals and results it wants to obtain. It is these goals and measures that will define for every employee, investor, vendor, and regulator what "success" means for the company. These goals give direction for decision-making and guide performance and behaviors. The clearer our articulation of these goals and metrics is, the more able our company will be to remain focused on those activities that lead to good results.

"Achievement" can mean profit and its related goals. Employee or customer satisfaction may be the key result an organization may look for. Brand or market dominance could be the goal. Other firms may seek more altruistic objectives. Whatever the case, companies need to specify the desired results and manage to them. Goal formulation options will be detailed further later in this chapter.

Putting It All Together

So what does a mission statement look like? For Adobe, the publishing software company, all the elements that we've discussed come together, as follows, in its mission statement and values:

Adobe's Mission

To be the premier provider of award-winning software solutions for network publishing, including Web, print, video, wireless, and broadband applications, in the company's addressed market segments while:
- Achieving and maintaining an above-average return on investment for shareholders measured in terms of return on equity, earnings per share, revenue growth, and operating profit.
- Maintaining or achieving the number one or two position in addressed market segments in terms of market share, customer satisfaction, revenue generation, product margin, product functionality, and technology leadership.
- Treating all employees with respect and rewarding both group and

individual performance that exceeds commitments and expectations.
- Being a good corporate citizen in the local and national locations where the company produces, sells, and services its products.

Values and Beliefs
- Conduct business on the highest ethical basis.
- Thrive on innovation.
- Treat people as you would like to be treated.
- For our customers
  - Deliver the best and most innovative products.
  - License technology on a fair and impartial basis.
  - Maintain total confidentiality about each customer's business.
  - Provide the highest level of service.
- For our employees
  - Hire the best and treat them well.
  - Provide a first-class working environment.
  - Offer the opportunity to participate in the ownership and economic success of the company.
- For our shareholders
  - Provide a superior return through growth and careful husbanding of our resources.
- For our community
  - Support charitable causes and public-benefit programs.
  - Provide a good example of progressive employment and business practices.

Don't these words paint a vibrant picture of this company? That is a vision. We can see clearly what's important and measured and how the company's philosophy operates with its various constituencies. Adobe sums up its business idea with this catchy vision, "Publish anything, anywhere, on any device." And by the way, Adobe ranked fifth on the *Fortune* "100 Best Companies to Work For" survey in 2003.

What Can We Learn from Adobe's Vision?

Here are a few observations about the Adobe mission and values statements that should help you construct your own vision.

First, it emphasizes product excellence and innovation. Adobe clearly wants "award-winning" products seen as the best in the industry.

Second, the company references often the concept of "addressed market segments." This implies that the company knows which segments it wants to service and which it does not want to attack.

Third, Adobe places achievement first in its mission: goals drive strategy.

Notice that, importantly, Adobe specifies the measures it will use to define success. Return on equity, earnings per share, revenue growth, and operating profit are very important. Market leadership (number one or two) in share, satisfaction, and the other measures mean that the company strives to dominate its competition.

On the other hand, we might question whether Adobe has too many metrics in its list, so that it's not apparent which are most important. Only management can clarify that situation.

Fourth, notice how important employee satisfaction and workplace ideals are to this company. Since software development is so much a people-driven business, getting and keeping smart developers is critical to success; the company knows it and believes in it.

Fifth, customers get innovation, fair treatment, excellent service, and privacy. Fair licensing does not necessarily mean, however, low prices; for market dominance, innovation, and great service, customers must pay and generate an above-average return to Adobe shareholders.

Finally, the company wants to be seen as a good citizen, in all its markets. If you're going to be the "big dog" (number one or two), Adobe thinks that it's good practice to also give back to those markets, visibly.

Organizational Goals That Make Sense

If we need goals to influence behavior and develop strategy, how do we choose which goals are best for our company? Let's begin with the most fundamental goal for a business: *maximize the value of the firm to the shareholders.*

Creating value, then, is the ultimate business goal. Each company, however, must decide how explicitly it's going to create value for the various groups in its sphere of influence. Some companies limit the business objective to creating value for shareholders. The assumption here is that we cannot create value for the owners unless we are also creating value for the customers and others. In a competitive marketplace, we need

> **Key Term**
>
> **Value** The worth of something, as compared with its cost. This is a critical term in business management: firms create value for customers, shareholders, employees, and communities. For customers, it's when our product or service delivers something more than its price. For shareholders, it's when returns on investment exceed comparable investments. For employees, it's when the total benefits of a job (pay, benefits, satisfaction, self-worth) exceed the time, expertise, and effort that they invest. For communities, it's when the economic benefits (taxes, economic activity) and other benefits (philanthropy, good schools, and image) of the firm exceed the costs of having the company as a neighbor (traffic congestion, political influence, and pollution).

not explicitly be concerned about employees or customers or anyone else, since we would not be able to deliver value for shareholders unless we took reasonable care of the other groups. Firms that are managed for shareholders only can be called *financially driven*.

In their book, *Value Based Management,* John D. Martin and J. William Petty make the case for the shareholder value maximization principle as follows:

> Managers create shareholder value by identifying and undertaking investments that earn returns greater than the firm's cost of raising money. When they do this, there is an added benefit to society. Competition among firms for funds to finance their investment attracts capital to the best projects, and the entire economy benefits. This is Adam Smith's invisible hand at work in the capital markets.

Firms that are financially focused look to returns on equity, the stock price, and the factors that influence stock price, like earnings and earnings growth. In their goal statements, profit and return-related measures dominate. Other firms take a different approach.

At CDW, everything revolves around the customer. Companies like CDW are *customer-focused* and believe that value to all the relevant groups will be enhanced if the customers benefit. The focus is on the business idea, the transaction, the unmet needs that the company is satisfying. Customer-focused firms will look to goals like market share, customer satisfaction, repeat customers, and revenue growth measures.

Since neither the shareholders nor the customers actually conduct any of the business for the company, some firms are *employee-focused*. These organizations believe that all value is created by the employees and through the employees. For these firms, goals relate to employee satisfaction, retention, education, and well-being. Service businesses and knowledge businesses tend to be more employee-focused, since the link between the business and value creation lies directly with the employees. Edward Jones is an employee-centered company.

Each organization needs to plainly articulate to everyone what its priorities are with respect to goals and measures of success. As we have seen, firms differ dramatically in their emphases, but ultimately a company must set its priorities relative to its business idea, its markets, its philosophy of doing business, and its purpose. Whatever our choice, however, our goals must be clear and well communicated and they must make a difference in daily decision-making. It's critical that decision makers know the relative importance of value creation to owners, customers, employees, and community, so that the vision of the firm can be attained. Just like *Alice in Wonderland*, Yogi Berra realized the vital importance of goal setting when he said, "You've got to be careful if you don't know where you're going, 'cause you might not get there."

Manager's Checklist for Chapter 2

❑ We cannot even begin to think of strategy until we have objectives.

❑ A corporate vision is a picture of the organization in 10-20 years.

❑ Vision is composed of goals, purpose, and values.

❑ Goals need to be prioritized based on our business, markets, and how value is created. We must clearly state our priorities for all constituencies of the organization. We must clearly state our measures of success.

❑ Our mission statement captures our organization's purpose. We should consider products, customers, markets, philosophy of doing business, and achievement in this important document.

❑ Firms with formal acknowledgment of their vision do better than those without such a written statement. Of course, successful firms actually live their vision in their actions.

❑ Companies tend to be financially driven, customer-focused, or employee-focused. Successful firms choose among these and communicate how trade-offs are decided when there are conflicts.

Reference

Charles Rarick and John Vitton, "Mission Statements Make Cents," *Journal of Business Strategy*, 16, (1995), 11. Also, Christopher K. Bart and Mark C. Baetz, "The Relationship Between Mission Statements and Firm Performance: An Exploratory Study," *Journal of Management Studies*, 35 (1998), 823-853.

A Strategy Road Map

Anyone who has watched the first 20 minutes of Steven Spielberg's film, *Saving Private Ryan,* is awestruck by the courage and grit of the men who stormed the beaches at Normandy on D-Day. The D-Day invasion was the critical battle of the war in Europe during World War II. But the victory was not won because the Allies sent thousands of men onto the beach June 6, 1944.

Winning that battle required extreme bravery by the thousands of troops, but also a comprehensive and coordinated plan of attack that would maximize the probability of a successful outcome.

In his book, *D-Day,* Stephen Ambrose described the details of that battle plan, called Overlord. That plan took more than two years for Eisenhower and his staff to develop and included sending paratroops behind enemy lines before the invasion; precise naval and air bombardments; wave after wave of invading infantry, armor, and artillery; the destruction of German transportation and communication capabilities; and hundreds of other activities, timed exactly, focused on achieving the objective of establishing a position from which the Allies could retake the Nazi-occupied territory in Europe. The ultimate objective was to take Berlin and oust Hitler.

How are such complex and important strategies developed? Is there a process that managers can follow to construct plans for business success to maximize the probability of a successful outcome? Yes. In this chapter we'll detail the steps of that process for constructing successful business strategies.

Where Is Strategy Born?

If we have a good business idea and some goals, we can begin to craft a strategy for our business. Unfortunately, because we have many decisions to make, it can be difficult to find a starting point. Figure 3-1 outlines a model for the strategic process, that is, a road map for building a strategy, which will serve as a guide to our discussion in this chapter.

Strategy development is focused on the answers to three important questions, which are framed at the bottom of the diagram.

First, *Where are we now?* Whether we're a start-up company with new products, services, or business ideas or a multi-national corporation in business for a century, the starting place is an in-depth assessment of the current situation and a thoughtful review of important trends that influence our business. The objective is to determine really fundamental questions about customers, markets, regulation, competition, and economic activity, now and in the future. In this analysis, it's important how comprehensive and analytical our research is, but also our success depends on how good our answers are, particularly regarding the most important aspects of our business.

The second question in formulating strategy is *Where should we go?* These are our business ideas. In framing the answers to this question, our objective is to develop a number of strategic alternatives and select the best choice. Of course,

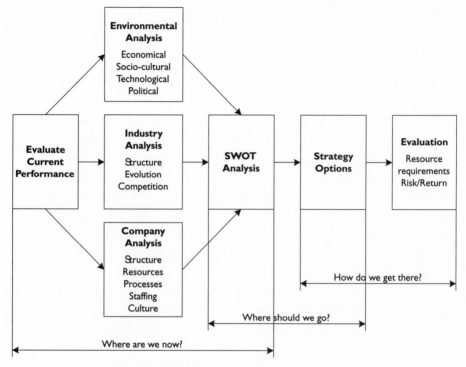

Figure 3-1. The process for developing strategy

our options will be based on our current situation, our goals, and our analysis of the alternatives that make sense. For example, if our objective is to increase revenue, our strategic alternatives may be to lower prices in order to increase volumes, increase distribution channels (adding Internet distribution, for example), or add geographies or customer segments. The process proposed here is that each alternative is identified and then analyzed and ultimately a decision is reached about the selected strategies.

The final question is *How do we get there?* This question is critical to address in detail.

Let's suppose, for example, that in our example above, we choose to add a customer segment in order to increase revenue. In this step of the process, we need to implement a whole series of actions in order to reach our revenue targets. In this case, we would be attempting to reach a new segment about which we may know little.

One place to start would be market research into the unmet needs that we would be satisfying. But, importantly, we would have to redesign or reposition our products/services to meet the new customer wants and needs. Second, we would have to understand distribution and then take action to reach the new segment. Further, many other actions would be needed to effectively market and service our products in a new segment. Of course, we must do all of this in a way that does not cannibalize our current customers. The implementation step may also call for organizational or structural changes and certainly will require new management systems, including assessment mechanisms to evaluate the new strategic direction.

It's naïve to think of these three questions and processes as independent, however. A key to a successful strategic initiative is to integrate these assessments, choices, and actions in order to reach the ultimate corporate objectives. Remember: the objective is to determine a strategy that will be successful. In the remainder of this chapter, we will explore each of these three questions and the methods by which we can answer them.

Evaluating Current Performance

The first step in strategy formulation is to assess the current performance of the organization. In most organizations, current performance is checked very regularly, but, in general, monthly (weekly or daily) reports are used to modify operational activities. For example, if sales were down relative to expectations for two months, prices might be lowered to promote more activity.

In a strategic review, performance analysis takes on a different meaning. In this context, performance evaluation is considered in a bigger time frame and with respect to the major goals and strategic initiatives of the organization.

For example, in a strategic review we might find that the

Gap Analysis

With 2:30 left in the game, the Denver Broncos were down 9 points to the Cleveland Browns. "All we need is a touchdown and a field goal, boys—no problem," John Elway, the Denver quarterback, calmly told his teammates in the huddle. That was a gap analysis.

This tool simply compares our current performance level and the desired performance level and then determines what that performance differential means. If our return on sales is at 6% and we expect to be able to deliver 8%, the difference is obviously 2%. Gap analysis then explores what key factors are driving the shortfall and what levels of performance are required to fill the gap. We might find that the missing 2%, for example, is principally driven by weak receivables performance and so we will shore up our credit policy, factor the receivables to convert them to cash, and outsource collections more aggressively. Gap analysis finds the link between performance deficiencies and the factors under our control that can be adjusted to fill the gap.

trend in sales is up significantly over the last two years, even though the current experience in sales is down. We might reason that the overall sales are on target because of our strategic plan to renovate all of our stores and that recent experience is a matter of economic conditions that will be corrected by pricing adjustments. Of course, we would base our conclusions on the data available in these matters. For example, we would compare carefully the sales trends at renovated stores and older, unchanged stores to determine whether that initiative is indeed driving more business.

Performance should always be measured relative to something else. We may compare ourselves with historical measures, our goals, our competitors, and our customers' expectations. The measures we select to evaluate our performance will depend on our objectives.

For example, suppose we have revenue objectives that are consistent with our long-term vision for the organization. If revenue is growing each year (historical comparison) at moderate rates, we may be satisfied, particularly if we've reached the rev-

Keys to the Vault

Smart Managing There is an old adage in business, "measure what you manage." Finding the right metrics for our firm, given its situation in the marketplace, is absolutely critical to our success. We must balance between being too comprehensive (too many things to measure) and too precise (too few). You'll find that if you select the correct measurement tools and make them known (communicate them) and important (link part of personal objectives to compensation), results will follow.

In order to find the right measures, though, we must look at the real drivers of our business. If, for example, we are a low-margin business and our goal is to produce a certain profit level or rate of return, we probably must look closely at our important costs of doing business and benchmark them against the best in the business. If our goals are sales-oriented, we might look to sales (units and revenue) per sales expenditures. Even further, we might look to sales per salesperson and support staff or sales per market segment.

enue targets (goals) in our plan. However, if our closest competitors, either the ones we're concerned with or maybe the ones that Wall Street uses as our peer group, have double the growth of our firm, then we may not be creating enough value for customers or shareholders. Also, as our revenue grows, we must inquire about our level of customer satisfaction, which may be a key reason why we're losing share to our competitors.

Once we determine the level of our current performance, it's important to make the right comparisons. Ideally we would like to have *best practices* standards for each metric that we've chosen. These are the best performance results for companies like ours. For example, we might find one company that has the best level of return on equity and another company that shows the best level of return on sales. Obviously, these constitute the optimal levels of performance across our list of important criteria.

In summary, our assessment of our current performance should follow some logical steps:

1. Know our goals and current strategy.
2. Determine the critical, key drivers of our business goal achievement.

Benchmarking

When we want to compare ourselves with competitors and strategic peers, how do we do it? Many sources of information are available to find comparable metrics.

For publicly traded companies, Web sites like www.sec.gov/edgar.shtml provide access to SEC documents like 10-Qs and 10-Ks. These corporate financial reports provide a wealth of information. 10-Qs and 10-Ks also include a section called "Management's Discussion and Analysis of Financial Condition and Results of Operations," which assesses the results for the year or quarter. A careful reading of this material will often yield valuable information about the company and its operations.

Another good source of data is financial analysts' reports on the company and the industry. Most large brokerage houses provide reports on companies that they follow. These reports also track key non-financial information that's important to the future value of the businesses.

Trade associations also provide limited information about the companies in their industry.

Finally, there are benchmarking firms that specialize in producing comparative data; in fact, often the large accounting and consulting shops have a benchmarking practice.

Regardless of the source, be sure to check the composition of ratios and measures that are used, so that accurate comparisons can be made with your company formula for the same item.

3. Identify the correct measure of each of the key drivers.
4. Determine the levels of our performance on each of the measures, compared with
   - Our historical performance over time
   - Our objectives
   - Our key competitors
   - Our customers' expectations
   - Best practices in the business
5. Synthesize these findings into an assessment of our current situation through gap analysis and a critical review of our activities, in each area, that have led to our results.

CAUTION!

Apply Common Sense to Best Practices

It's important to remember that a company's performance is directly related to its strategy. In using best practices, it's common for these metrics to become targets—and this is not necessarily a good thing. One company may be the leader in an important measure, such as speed to market for new products. In comparing our company with the leader, however, we must also consider the factors that led to its superior results. The company with the best speed to market may believe in a first-mover advantage and so may have invested heavily in research and the new product development process. Therefore, its performance level probably cannot be a target for our company, if we don't share that first-to-market strategy and our levels of investment are not comparable. If our strategy is directed at a specific market segment or sales through enhanced branding, we could not duplicate that speed-to-market experience.

On the other hand, this kind of explanatory evaluation of performance levels should not be an excuse to dismiss benchmarking. We may still determine that our speed to market can be improved significantly and we should use these facts that we uncover through analysis to assess how we might bridge the gap between our performance and our strategic success.

Environmental Analysis

If nothing ever changed in our world and markets, then we could rely on adjustments to current performance to map future strategy. But that's not the case. So we use an analysis of our environment (and the next step, an analysis of our industry) to get a better picture of the business circumstances that we'll face in the future—the place where our new strategies will be implemented.

Environmental analysis consists of looking at the factors within the social, economic, political, regulatory, and technological climates that affect our business, both today and in the future. The purpose is to understand how trends and/or changes in these various factors will influence and affect our operations. Most business enterprises are linked with these kinds of factors to one degree or another, and therefore, a careful analysis will assist in the planning for future strategic development.

Social Factors

One of the most important social factors to consider is the impact of demographic trends on our business. Demographics are characteristics of the population, such as age, gender, race, ethnicity, income, education, location, and occupation.

Environmental analysis
A methodical examination of the factors within the social, economic, political, regulatory, and technological contexts in which a business operates.

Here's a simple example of how demographics can help us formulate strategy. Consider a toy company like Mattel. Mattel's business is driven by birth rates and the growth (positive or negative) of the population in the youth age brackets, like 6-10 years or 11-13 years. Mattel's principal toy, the Barbie doll, is largely attractive to girls aged 7-12, so this is an important demographic factor for the company to consider.

Demographic issues influence many, if not all, businesses. As discussed briefly earlier in the book, the Baby Boomers (born between 1946 and 1956) have a great impact on all economic activity. As the first Baby Boomers age toward 60 years, their power in the marketplace is felt in any area in which their buying habits are affected. For example, the Sunbelt can expect a surge in second or retirement home purchases. Drug companies, both over-the-counter and prescription, clearly are expecting more business.

Gender is another significant factor. Women have been decision makers in health care and family-related purchases for a long time. As women have entered the workforce in greater numbers, their influence in financial matters has also increased significantly; marketers from financial services companies have noticed and responded to this influence. Car manufacturers have also begun to cater to women as decision makers; in fact, GM's Saturn Division designed some of its practices to be attractive to female buyers. Lowe's and Home Depot are in intense competition in the market for home and garden products. According to

---

Sources of Demographic Information

Demographic information can be found in a number of sources. A popular and easy to use resource is the *Statistical Abstract of the United States*. This book is published annually by the Bureau of the Census and can be found in most libraries. The book provides a wealth of statistical information on demographic and economic issues, and can be used to prompt further research. Another valuable demographic resource is the census bureau Web site, www.census.gov. This site provides not only facts about current demographics, but also trends for the future.

---

the popular and finance press, Lowe's stores are more attractive to women, so they've gained in market share.

As these examples demonstrate, understanding how demographic trends shape future markets and the demand for our products is quite important. We should analyze the demographic categories that are most influential to our business. For some businesses, the growing Hispanic populations provide new opportunities; for others, the rise of the African-American middle class has been noteworthy. Whatever the case, understanding demographic trends is important to developing strategic plans.

Economic Factors

At the heart of strategic planning is the understanding of what economic circumstances our organization will face in the future. While the factors will vary from business to business, every company will need to understand the business cycle. The U.S. economy moves in waves between economic growth and recession. Knowing where we are in the cycle and where we are going is critical to business decision-making. Interest rates, unemployment rates, and factors such as energy costs and health care costs all contribute to the economic picture at any time. And each of these factors is subject to trends.

The easiest example of economic analysis contributing to a company's strategic thinking is that, as interest rates rise, housing activity falls. So, for example, when interest rates are rising, a furniture store might think twice about expanding its show-

Sources of Economic Information

When looking at economic data there are lots of resources that are readily available. One source that is particularly useful is the Department of Commerce's Web page, www.stat-usa.gov. On this one site, the federal government provides up-to-date information on the following topics: consumer and producer prices, GDP growth, housing, employment, retail and other sales data, interest rates, foreign currency exchange rates, and country research. This site is a powerhouse for economic analysis.

room. Also, look at what rising oil prices in the 1970s did for the small car market in the United States.

Over the last few iterations of the business cycle an interesting phenomenon has occurred in the U.S. economy, that is, cycles by regions. New England, for example, might experience a longer deeper recession than other parts of the country. The Southwest might not experience much of a recession at all. Obviously, given this experience our exposure to different geographical regions would impact our planning.

Geography also plays a part in the dynamics of global businesses. For example, Japan has experienced a 10-year economic down period, including deflation. The impact of exchange rates, prices of goods, and import-export activity will all play an important role in determining the strategic direction of our company. As a result, a good look at current and potential foreign economic conditions and trends can prove to be extremely valuable.

Economic analysis is like getting a weather report before we go off to play golf. What should we wear? Should we bring the umbrella? Will the wind be strong and in our face all day—or at our backs? We will still need to do the detailed analysis of our own markets, but understanding the economic conditions will prepare our strategies for the correct circumstances.

Political and Regulatory Factors

One of the great secrets in business is that governmental changes—legislative, legal, or regulatory—create tremendous

Sources of Regulatory and Political Information

Information on legal proposals and judicial rulings is usually one of the main benefits of affiliating with a trade association. In most cases, these organizations keep their members apprised about such issues through newsletters and meetings.

However, it's not enough to be aware of these proposals and issues. Your company must have a systematic mechanism for considering the impact of the proposals, both in the present and for the future.

opportunities for new business ideas. As an example, the federal government passed a piece of legislation in 1996 called the Health Insurance Portability and Accountability Act (HIPAA). The intent of the bill was to alleviate some of the problems associated with small businesses in the purchase of health insurance. A part of the bill also addressed the privacy of health information for all health care institutions: insurers, providers, and service companies. The privacy component was a small part of the law, and its implementation was delayed for a few years. Some astute observers of HIPAA in the health business anticipated the huge impact on operations and technology that the implementation would require, and created business units to address the unmet needs of the health care system, and have reaped the benefits.

The lesson of HIPAA for strategy decision-makers is to stay current on proposed legislation, rather than merely complain about potential increased government regulation or interference, and to look for the business opportunities. Not all governmental changes will favor growth of businesses; sometimes businesses will lose value because of new laws or rulings and management may need to consider reducing or even dropping products or services. Those who keep current on political and regulatory factors will be able to make wiser decisions earlier and minimize the damages.

Technological Factors

Technology is affecting business more and more: no company can afford to neglect technological factors in its environmental analysis. A few examples will be enough to make this point.

A lot of money has been made and lost—maybe mostly lost—betting on the Internet as a tool of business. However, there's no doubt that the Internet has had a serious impact on how companies conduct their business, now and even more in the future. Also, what about cell phones, e-mail, and PDAs? And think about the digitization of documents and pictures. And not all technology is electronic: consider the materials being used in common objects all around us—metal alloys, plastics for everything from beverage containers to car parts, and recycled materials of all sorts. Finally, reflect on the perfection, application, and growth of the laser, used in CD and DVD players for music and films and as a substitute for scalpels in eye surgery and for reading bar codes on virtually everything we buy. In short, technology changes the status quo, in profound and dramatic ways.

The music business, for instance, struggles with new technology. While CDs replaced albums and tapes, the music business model is threatened by the digitization of music and the applications of software that permits transferring songs through computers. The Web site Napster was shut down by the legal action of the music industry because Napster completely bypassed the business system that pays artists and music companies for their creations. Similar sites have evolved. Technology advances will probably continue to challenge the music business model, so firms in the music industry must find new strategies.

Building a strategy requires that we consider how technology will affect our business: products, services, processes, and investment. However, technology assessment is difficult. Many new technologies come to the market for new applications at great cost and often deliver only a portion of the expected benefits. Firms must balance the promise of new technology with the investment level and the benefits of competitive advantage that they may or may not realize with early adoption of the technology. Again, these are hard calls to make and require a comprehensive approach, across all functional areas, to be successful.

Industry Analysis

While environmental analysis scans the trends and changes in economic, social, and other factors, industry analysis looks specifically at the markets in which a company competes. In industry analysis, the focus is split between the current state of these markets and the future. Doing an industry review is an important component of preparing the groundwork for developing strategy. Industry analysis is broken down into three components: structure, evolution, and competition.

Structure

The first question that we need to address is: what industry? Companies that share the basic product/market mix define industries. So, for example, retail sales are differentiated from business-to-business sales.

Once we know what industry we want to analyze, we begin with structure issues. These are the following:

- size (revenues and/or units)
- growth rate and trends
- number of competitors and market share (concentration)
- number, type, and concentration of buyers
- distribution channels used

SIC Codes

Standard Industry Classification codes have been used since the 1930s in the United States. Each company is assigned a code that represents the industry grouping that best aligns with its business. There are 11 broad classifications and hundreds of detailed classifications. The 11 broad industry groupings are: agricultural, forestry and fishing; mining; construction; manufacturing; transportation and public utilities; wholesale trade; retail trade; finance, insurance and real estate; services; public administration; and nonclassifiable establishments. These codes, in varying levels of detail, are very useful in organizing companies into industry groupings. For a complete listing of SIC codes, go to www.wave.net/upg/immigration/sic_index.html.

The Work Is Already Done—Sort Of

One trick for getting someone else to do your industry analysis is to look to the publicly traded companies in the industry.
In most cases, the large brokerage firms have research analysts who prepare industry studies on a regular basis. So create the list of all the public companies that are in your industry; then look them up on Yahoo! Finance (finance.yahoo.com) or some other site to find which brokerage houses cover the companies. A phone call to a few of these analysts should yield a study or two on your industry—already done.

Beware of relying on these research reports as your sole source of information because they may deal with only a few companies in the industry. But usually their analysis can be very helpful in creating a picture of our industry.

- entry and exit barriers
- industry profitability and trends
- stock market performance of publicly traded companies

The objective of the industry analysis is to get a complete picture of the activities taking place in the markets that we serve. Industry analysis gives us a 30,000-foot view of the companies and results of the players in our field.

Industry Evolution

Understanding the history and trends of an industry, can help us determine where the companies and customers are going. Through this process, we can judge how our firm will lead or react in order to sustain our position and achieve success. Again Wayne Gretsky's advice is to go where the puck will be is important. Anticipation can lead to goals in

What Is a Competitor?

Smart Managing

Here is a definition of a competitor that I really like. Karl Albrecht, in an excellent book called *Corporate Radar*, about the analysis that goes into formulating strategy, gives the following definition. Albrecht says that a competitor is "any entity that offers options to your customers which can diminish the appeal of the options you offer." This great definition immediately gets you thinking about any entity and the comparative appeal of your products.

hockey, and attainment of goals in business.

Michael Porter in his book, *Competitive Strategy,* outlined five forces affecting industries that can provide a framework for looking at industry evolution. By exploring each of these items, we can better find the future of our industry, its competitors, and customers. The five forces are:

- bargaining power of consumers
- potential for substitute products
- bargaining power of suppliers
- entry of new competitors
- rivalry among competitors

Consumer power is rising in most markets because of global competition and the Internet as a source of product and price information. As more countries develop around the world, more competitors are created, which fuels more competition for market share. Look at the arrival of Korean companies into U.S. markets for electronics and cars, for example.

With these new choices, consumers have more power to leverage prices and product features with existing firms. Add to the mix the power of the Internet for adding transparency to the marketplace. This transparency really does make the promise of competitive markets—perfect information between buyers and sellers—more of a reality. As a result, consumers possess broader and deeper knowledge in the market, and knowledge is power.

Substitute products can put our entire company, and industry at risk. To gauge the evolution of our industry, it's vital that we monitor the potential for substitute products emerging that threaten our line. Try to find a typewriter today! There is no better example of substitute products, PCs, destroying an industry that was vibrant just 20 years ago.

Supplier power needs to be evaluated. As power intensifies in the hands of a few suppliers, product differentiation becomes more difficult, and pricing becomes market share dependent. Microsoft has become the dominant operating system supplier to the PC industry. So much so that the Justice Department brought its anti-trust unit after some of Microsoft's practices, and product strategies. In examining the evolution of our industry, it is important to look at the momentum that suppliers have in the marketplace. As suppliers consolidate, our risk increases, particularly if we are a smaller player.

Entry of competitors is a trend factor that is important to follow. When new competitors enter an industry, they target either profit or customers. Either way it is bad for the existing players. Those industries with good profit margins are targets for potentially all other companies. If the new competitors are well capitalized, they can win over market share with pricing. Alternatively, new entrants might be looking to secure a customer base through related products or services and get better results through a larger share of each customer's wallet. Many insurance companies are adding banking services (for example, State Farm) to better secure their clientele from banks, which are aggressively moving into insurance markets.

Finally, all these factors present themselves as rivalry among firms in an industry. Some of these are comparable to those in sports: Pepsi versus Coke, Ford versus GM, Crest versus Colgate, and many others dominate their industry's competitive scene. Seeing these trends before they actualize permits good companies to craft strategies that reflect marketplace realities and preserve good business for themselves.

Competition

The next level of analysis in the market is of competitors. Now we are getting to a 1,000-foot view of the market, focusing on individual competitors. The basic questions that we want answered by this work are the following:

- Who are the key competitors?
- Are there competitors we're not thinking about because they're just beginning to enter our product/market space?
- What are our competitors doing?
- Which competitors can we attack? What is the best

TRICKS OF THE TRADE

Finding Competitive Information
One of the best places to find out what competitors are planning is to monitor the employment want ads. Through the want ads, you can see what investments companies are making. New locations, expansions, new systems, and new marketing approaches all can be inferred by the nature of the people that the competitor is looking to hire. It's not rocket science, but it's a good look into your competitors' business plans. And it's free and easy to do. An updated version of this tactic is to check the "career opportunities" section of your competitors' Web sites.

approach?
• Which competitors should we defend against? Where are we vulnerable?

Competitive analysis is not a one-shot deal. Good companies constantly and consistently have their collective ears to the ground using every source of information: sales people, customers, suppliers, government agencies (which frequently have a lot of information, depending upon the type of business), news reports, and (of course!) the Internet. Good competitive analysis is good spy work: stealthy, accurate, and timely.

Internal Analysis

We've just outlined the methods and issues associated with a rigorous external analysis of the environment and our markets. More will be detailed on these topics in later chapters. Now we return to an assessment of our own organization. Remember that the process began with a performance review, looking at our company's results on the dimensions that we determined are important and linked with our goals. Now we'll look at our company in terms of structure, resources, and culture. This internal review, when combined with the other analysis that has been suggested, will permit us to develop strategies that will allow us to achieve the identified objectives and recognize the trends and other important factors both inside and outside the firm.

Structure

Strategists need to be completely familiar with the organizational structure. A good look at our activities, processes, and relationships is useful, particularly as we identify performance results that need attention. The classic example is the hierarchical firm in which cost levels are too high. By reducing bureaucracy and empowering employees, many firms can realize tremendous efficiencies in operations.

Another good example of the importance of knowing the structure for executing good strategy is the case in which divestiture is considered. Later on in this book, we'll explore why firms may choose to sell pieces of their operations, but prior to the sale, structural issues are critical. The principal structural concern is whether we can separate the operations from the rest of our firm and at what cost. Selling a particular business unit seems easy enough, but what if virtually all of the staff functions of the unit are performed by units elsewhere in the company and not for sale? Prior to divestiture, we must ready the entity structurally, as well as financially.

Resources

As we consider developing strategies for the future, we must consider and evaluate the current resources of the organization and the resources required by new initiatives. In particular, the resource evaluation is an examination of the assets of the company: people, property, and relationships. In a later chapter, we'll explain the asset review method of strategy development that uses our current assets as the key determinant of future strategy.

In this stage we're asking basic questions about the available resources of the company. Here are some examples:

- How good are our people?
  - At sales?
  - At innovation?
  - At operations?

- How good is our technology?
  - At delivering productivity?
  - What is our system's capacity?
- Do we have access to capital?
- Are we delivering value to customers, shareholders, and employees?

The process for reviewing resources is quite simple. First, make a list of the important resources that the organization requires to be successful. Usually this is done by category (people, property, relationships). Second, make a list of the key departments or areas of the organization that are critical to delivering successful results: sales, R&D, operations, finance, engineering—whatever is relevant to the business. Finally, do an assessment based on results, trends, competitors, management judgments, or the facts as we see them. This review allows us to determine our internal strengths and weakness, categorized by the key areas of our business (processes, staffing, investment, management). This analysis leads directly into the next step of the strategy road map, SWOT analysis.

> **SWOT analysis** Examination of strengths, weaknesses, opportunities, and threats. This review and its results are a foundation for the formulation of strategic alternatives. SWOT is a byproduct of the internal and external reviews that we have been discussing.

Culture

Before we move to that next step, there's one more aspect of our internal analysis to review: culture. The term "organizational culture" has become commonly used, maybe even overly used, but what does it mean?

The dimensions of culture include items like pace, focus, aggressiveness in competition, community involvement, entrepreneurship, risk taking, and management style in decision making. Understanding our culture is important, particularly as

Culture, Nordstrom Style

We all know a strong culture when we feel it. Walk into a Nordstrom store. Most of the time you will hear a piano playing, there will be an ample number of employees to help you, and the shoe department will knock your socks off. There's a certain feel that Nordstrom has cultivated over a long time. The feel of a Nordstrom store is a customer's view of culture, but typically such a feel is the result of building a culture from an employee's point of view. As a consequence, customers and employees expect a certain type and level of service that helps define the Nordstrom shopping experience.

we develop new strategies and contemplate change. For example, if we consider a strategy for growth that includes acquiring other firms in the industry, recognizing the cultural differences becomes vitally important to the success of the transaction. Cultural differences in risk taking and style may be reflected in pay systems. One firm may base a heavy component of total compensation on performance measures, while another may base only a modest amount on such measures. These pay systems reflect the cultural differences of the organizations and, therefore, should be weighed heavily in building expectations in the merged company.

So Where Are We Now?

The strategy road map that we are building is a process to determine the direction that the organization will take to achieve its objectives. Our first step is to evaluate where we are now, by doing the following:

- Evaluate current and historical performance, using a variety of comparison measures.
- Do an environmental analysis of economic, social, political, and technological facts and trends.
- Analyze our industry to uncover the trends and potential and study our competitors.
- Examine our company's structure, resources, and culture.

Assessment Is Ongoing

Many companies that do strategic planning make this exercise a yearly procedure. These firms may have an off-site meeting, produce binders filled with analysis, and carefully lay out the strategies for the next five years and the plans to implement those strategies. Often, however, those binders are filed on bookshelves, never to be opened again.

The performance review and external and internal analyses described here should be ongoing processes. Good companies create a system in which new information about the environment, the industry, or the company can be updated and assessed on a regular basis in the context of the strategic plan.

The responsibility for managing the strategic process clearly falls with top management. As new information about competitor activities is learned, as regulatory changes unfold, or as economic conditions change, the managers need to know it, to incorporate the information into their database and the collective consciousness, and to review their strategies in light of the information. Good companies make strategy a regular part of their formal business activities and test what they know against what they do.

Strategy Formulation

After our analytical review, the next steps involve strategic thinking. By "strategic thinking" we mean using the information that we've collected to determine an answer to the question, where should we go? The recommended first step is SWOT analysis. From there, a number of techniques can be used to actually develop strategic options.

SWOT Analysis

SWOT is used to map the clear objectives of the organization to the strengths, weaknesses, opportunities, and threats that we can see based on our previous comprehensive data assessment. Notice that it's very important when evaluating the SWOT to always keep in mind the goals of the firm. Without that guidance, it's very easy for the SWOT result to get off track.

SWOT involves three steps, which are applied first to strengths, second to weaknesses, third to opportunities, and last to threats:

1. Systematically determine the strengths/weaknesses/ opportunities/threats of our business, in detail, based upon the facts and trends that we discovered in the strategic analysis portion of the process.
2. Match these strengths/weaknesses/opportunities/threats to achieving particular elements of the objectives.
3. Rank the strengths/weaknesses/opportunities/threats in order of importance to achieving our goals.

The most effective SWOT reviews include staff from many levels of the organization, to gain a well-rounded and grounded perspective. By compiling these lists of the top SWOT factors, the company is ready to apply strategic thinking to begin the process of formulating strategy.

Developing Strategy Options

There are many approaches that we'll use later in this book to develop the strategy options. Clearly, the SWOT analysis leads us to strategies, if we simply take actions to do the following:

- Build on our strengths.
- Shore up our weaknesses.
- Seize worthwhile opportunities.
- Defend against business threats.

While this is a good start, we can also use other techniques to find innovative and successful strategies to reach our goals. In this pursuit, we're beginning to address a new question: How do we get there?

Evaluate Options, Evaluate Results

The final step in the strategy road map is evaluation.

First, we need to evaluate the strategy options to determine which is or are best. The guiding principle here is the action or

Smart Managing

Do You Want to Improve the Strategic Planning Process?

Don't leave those pretty binders with the plans, estimates, and forecasted results on the shelf. Bring them out regularly and compare the assumptions, time frames, and the pro-forma financials with the real experience.

This approach of using the past work as a guide, by comparing the estimated data with the real thing, makes your company a learning organization. What did we know? What did we assume that went wrong? What changed? Address all of these questions, not to embarrass anyone but to learn and to make the process better the next time around. Most companies don't do this, but they should. You can make your firm better at strategy by keeping track of those five-year plans and learning from them.

actions with the best chance to achieve the stated goals and corporate vision.

Mapping out the strategy is not enough, however. Implementation of the strategy demands that we develop plans that extend throughout the organization. For example, if our strategy is to initiate and develop an Internet distribution system, then we lay out operating plans, timetables, and detailed work plans down and through the organization. We need to put into place technology investments, marketing initiatives, and fulfillment operations to make the strategy—the business idea—real.

Once we've decided on a course of action, then we must regularly monitor our progress and monitor the industry, environmental, and corporate changes, to determine whether the results are on track or off.

Good strategies anticipate changes in the environment. Good managers see the future and find a way to achieve their goals, through their strategies. Good companies learn from their experiences, both good and bad. We've laid out a road map for strategy development. Next, we'll explore each of these areas in detail.

Manager's Checklist for Chapter 3

❏ Management is a process and so is strategic management. Follow a systematic process for developing the strategic decisions of the company.

❏ External analysis looks at the environment and industry in which we work. Look for both facts and trends and know which factors truly drive your business.

❏ Assess your competition carefully.

❏ Internal analysis explores the current state of your business, including where the performance gaps lie. We also need to critically look at the operational state of our organization: resources, personnel, and culture.

❏ Formulate a SWOT report. For each category, rank the most important items, based on goals, so that as we develop new strategies, we can have the greatest impact.

❏ Bring a broad range of experiences, functions, and levels into the discussion of strategic choices. Make sure you can execute your strategy successfully.

❏ Evaluate choices and results, regularly and critically.

Customer Analysis

Jack Nicholson starred in an interesting movie in 1970 called *Five Easy Pieces.* In a classic restaurant scene, Nicholson's character is confronted with a culture that is neither customer-friendly nor accommodating. The dialogue goes like this:

Nicholson: I'd like a plain omelet, no potatoes, tomatoes instead, a cup of coffee, and wheat toast.

Waitress (pointing to the menu): No substitutions.

Nicholson: What do you mean? You don't have any tomatoes?

Waitress: *Only* what's on the menu. You can have a number two—a plain omelet. It comes with cottage fries and rolls.

Nicholson: Yeah, I know what it comes with. But it's not what I want.

Waitress: Well, I'll come back when you make up your mind.

Nicholson: Wait a minute. I have made up my mind. I'd like a plain omelet, no potatoes on the plate, a cup of coffee, and a side order of wheat toast.

Waitress: I'm sorry, we don't have any side orders of toast ... an English muffin or a coffee roll.

Nicholson: What do you mean you don't make side orders of toast? You make sandwiches, don't you?

Waitress: Would you like to talk to the manager?

Nicholson: You've got bread and a toaster of some kind?

Waitress: I don't make the rules.

Nicholson: OK, I'll make it as easy for you as I can. I'd like an omelet, plain, and a chicken salad sandwich on wheat toast, no mayonnaise, no butter, no lettuce. And a cup of coffee.

Waitress: A number two, chicken sal san, hold the butter, the lettuce, and the mayonnaise. And a cup of coffee. Anything else?

Nicholson: Yeah. Now all you have to do is hold the chicken, bring me the toast, give me a check for the chicken salad sandwich, and you haven't broken any rules.

Waitress (spitefully): You want me to *hold* the chicken, huh?

Well, we'll stop there, but as you can see this restaurant was not focused on satisfying the customer. Rather, the focus was on the convenience of the operations. Businesses can thrive even if they choose to be indifferent to the individual needs of their customers. But they must offer something else of value, such as price and/or exceptional, consistent quality.

McDonald's, like the restaurant of the film, discouraged substitutions from its sandwiches. It wasn't until Burger King came along to successfully woo customers with the "Have it your way" campaign that the dynamics of fast food customization were changed. Burger King found a way to meet an unmet need of its customers and it exploited that advantage to the detriment of its competitors.

Unmet customer needs are at the heart of business ideas and the development of business strategy. In this chapter we will

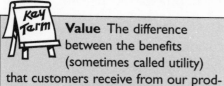

It's All About the Customers

Smart Managing   Successful businesses begin with the customers and meeting their unmet needs. Many people, both in the business world and outside, believe that business is about making money. Profit is a *result* of understanding and managing what customers expect, then delivering more. If we exceed their expectations, then we'll be able to price at a profit and make money. Monitoring and influencing the customer, however, must be a continuous part of our activities. Information technology's greatest benefit to business is to create a system for better understanding the customers and their needs.

explore an analysis of customers and their needs. We don't include this customer analysis as part of the strategy road map, although we could, because understanding our customers is not specific to developing strategy. Rather, it's an ongoing prerequisite of doing business and should be a regular part of management activities.

Basic Customer Questions

As we think about our business idea, the first issue to consider

Key Term   **Value** The difference between the benefits (sometimes called utility) that customers receive from our products or services and what customers pay for our products or services.

is the question, *What unmet customer needs are we targeting?* A fancier way to ask the question is *What is our value proposition?* Regardless of our business lingo sophistication, we need to know what we offer to customers in our products and/or services and how we propose to deliver value to them.

Steps in Customer Analysis

Simple common sense tells us that we need information in order to assess our business value proposition to customers. There are six inquiries that we need to develop in order to build a customer information database:

> ## Customer Needs and the Value Proposition
> Consider the purchase of a car. Buyers assess the factors, or benefits, that are important to them: room, safety, gas mileage, reliability, ease of purchase, trade-in value over time, and brand. Then they shop for the car that delivers those important features for the best price. If we can exceed their expectations of the benefits of owning our model, then we might hear them say something like "I got a lot of car for the money!" That defines value.
>
> Of course, value creation for the business occurs when we can sell the car for a price that exceeds our cost of delivering those important benefits to our customers.

1. Who are our customers?
2. Why do they buy from us?
3. Who buys from competitors?
4. Why do some buy from competitors?
5. Can we meet the needs of those buying from competitors, without sacrificing value to our customers?
6. What else can we do for our customers to create value for them and for ourselves?

Clearly, in order to answer these questions, we must know our customers and the markets well and we must develop methods for getting information from buyers and from nonbuyers. This information then becomes an input to our development of strategy.

Who Are Our Customers? Who Buys from Competitors?

Probably the easiest question to answer is to describe our current customers. Since we have records of their purchases, we can collect a variety of data. Registration cards included with products and invoice data are generally used to acquire this information. One way to approach growing our business is to identify our customers on a number of dimensions and then to assume that we are likely to appeal to other people of the same characteristics. Key characteristics differ depending on whether we're selling to individuals (B2C) or to businesses (B2B) or to both.

Key B2C characteristics:

- age
- sex
- lifestyle
- occupation
- geography
- frequency of purchase

Key B2B characteristics:

- type of organization
- size of organization
- geography
- frequency of purchase

Let's look at examples from each set.

Suppose we sell supplies to schools, a B2B example. We can categorize our customers by *type of organization*: elementary schools, junior high or middle schools, high schools, and colleges and universities.

The *size of the organization* is also an important characteristic to consider, particularly because the buying process may change as an organization grows. For example, large school entities may bid out all purchases and be more price-focused than smaller school entities. In bidding circumstances, relationships that are cultivated tend to be less important than other features, like convenience and price.

Geography, or location, also is an important factor to consider. In cases where location (states or regions) divides

TRICKS OF THE TRADE

Think Outside of the List

In analyzing customers, we might simply sort our current customer list by type. However, in doing this we may miss opportunities for exploring additional customers. Always think about all of the possible categories of organizations to which we might sell, even though we may not have any customers in a category.

In the schools example, the complete list might include preschools and day care centers, public versus private schools of all types, trade schools (like cosmetology or auto repair schools), technical colleges, and language institutes. By compiling a comprehensive list of possibilities, we get a better understanding of our penetration of the entire schools market and a more complete look at the potential for our business.

the sales reps, for example, location data becomes important in order to understand the customers, as well as judge the effectiveness of the sales force. Categorizing buyers into urban, suburban, or rural geographies is also valuable for differentiating their needs. For example, urban schools may require vastly different products (multilingual or multicultural materials) than rural or suburban schools. Finally, since many businesses face global competition as well as global opportunities, special consideration should be given to understanding foreign buyers.

Frequency of purchase is another good characteristic for understanding the buying habits and needs of our customers. Size of orders and regularity are important to inventory policy. For example, a school may place many small orders over the course of a year or one large order. Dividing our customers into classes of order size helps us to manage the ordering and fulfillment process to better meet the needs of our customers.

If our business is B2C, selling to individual consumers, our categories of interest are much different. Suppose we are selling golf equipment. We would want to know the differences in buying habits and needs by *age* and by *gender.* Clearly, equipment is differentiated by gender, so our stocking of goods is directly affected by our ability to merchandise effectively to each sex. Understanding our market by gender may lead us to conclude, for example, that we only want to serve female golfers, since they are underserved, have special needs, and are a growing market. The only way that we can intelligently make a decision like that is to have the information about these customers.

Lifestyle is particularly important to retail concerns, since in many ways the customers' needs are driven by their life activities. In the case of golf equipment, we would want to know whether our customers were country clubbers, play regularly at public courses, or are just occasional players. Since most clubs and courses have pro shops that sell merchandise and offer expertise, we would need to staff and stock our store differently based upon the lifestyle of the customers. Price and selection would depend upon the target customers that we attract.

> ## Better Than Par for the Course
>
> Nevada Bob's franchise store in Madison, Wisconsin is phe-
> nomenal. Over the years, the owner has attracted cus-
> tomers from nearly every segment of the golfing community to pur-
> chase hard and soft goods at his outlet. The inventory of goods is
> immense and customers throughout the region flock to the store for
> the latest and greatest in equipment, clothing, and supplies.
>
> Even country club members shop at Nevada Bob's because Joel
> Zucker, the owner, recognizes two important needs of serious players.
> First, they want to try the equipment. Second, they want a market for
> their used equipment. By filling both of these unmet needs, which pro
> shops generally do not meet, Nevada Bob's has become the preferred
> and dominant store in the market.

Occupation can be a useful characteristic in itself and it generally can be used as a surrogate for income. We would want to
know the golf budgets of our customers to help us offer goods
that are attractive.

Geography will be important as well. Are our customers willing to travel to shop at our stores? How far will our advertising
reach into the community before it becomes ineffective? These
questions are anticipated by understanding the customers who
would patronize our golf equipment store. We can also use the
data to identify any customers who may be celebrities in our
community. Oftentimes, retailers can use influential customers
for testimonials and create additional demand for their business.

Another important characteristic is *frequency of purchase.*
Some of our customers may buy frequently, others only sporad-
ically. If we know more about those customers who buy often,
we may unlock some effective marketing tools to develop other
customers into frequent buyers.

Regardless of the nature of our business and our customers,
it's critical to know as much about our customers as possible.
The first step is to group buyers into simple but powerful categories or segments, as described here, and use that information
to design business activities to maximize the results.

Why Do They Buy from Us? Why Do Some Buy from Competitors?

Once we know who are customers are, we would like to know more about their reasons for purchasing from us or not purchasing. If we know the features and qualities of our products or services that are attracting customers, we can market them more effectively. Getting this information is hard work, however.

When we develop our business idea, we usually think about designing features that will be attractive to consumers. These features and benefits are targeted at the buyers' unmet needs. In designing to meet these needs, we must ask and answer the question, *why do consumers buy our products or services, rather than not buying at all or buying from others?* Because the concept of meeting unmet needs is so central to successful marketing, monitoring the behaviors and rationale of our customers should be a major part of our ongoing marketing program.

How do we acquire this information and put it to use to more successfully define our offerings and strategy? There are a number of vehicles that we can use to gather customer information:

- point-of -sale information
- customer surveys
- focus groups

Point-of-Sale Information

Every time we have an interaction with a customer, we have an opportunity to learn more from the customer. In a sales call situation, whether a sale is made or not, the customer can tell us details about his or her needs and his or her reaction to our product features. In a service situation, the customer has had an opportunity to use the product and can give important feedback on the match between his or her needs and our features. It doesn't matter whether the sales or service circumstances are face to face with a person, at the checkout line or service center, or on the Internet, these events can provide a wealth of information for those companies that seize the opportunity and gather the data.

> ### Tapping into a Wealth of Information
>
> **Smart Managing** Software developers have recognized the valuable potential of customer interactions and offer many packages for collecting and organizing the information available. *Contact management* systems, like ACT (Best Software), permit input by salespeople from both customers (successful sales) and noncustomers. These systems permit organizations to categorize data on unmet needs, sales barriers, and comparisons with competitors. *Customer relationship management* (CRM) systems track behaviors of buyers and facilitate coordination of sales, service, and cross-selling opportunities. Siebel Systems, for example, provides a variety of CRM applications for B2B and B2C businesses. More information on both these systems can be found at their Web sites: www.act.com and www.siebel.com.

Point-of sale data also includes buyer behaviors. One of the best examples of using consumer behavior to deliver better results is in grocery stores. Vendors like General Mills and stores like Safeway can use scanning information to understand what product purchases get linked, such as beer and snack foods. Retailers can group goods that are commonly purchased together to make it more convenient for customers to choose these items. The net result is more revenue per customer.

> ### Tracking Buying Patterns
>
> **For Example** Take a closer look at the stocking practices in your grocery store. Notice how Frito-Lay has created little shelves for salsa and queso dips right there with the Fritos and Tostitos. Scanning the items permits analysts to see buying patterns much more clearly. The next time you go to the supermarket, take note of how the store tries to anticipate your needs.

Some companies turn anticipating customers needs into immediate revenue. If you order a book or music CD on www.amazon.com, the software running behind the site will often suggest other products that you might be interested in buying. If you're considering buying a book, for example, you may read that "customers who bought this book also bought ....," followed by a short list of titles based on the customer tracking system. This approach is not new in concept: for example, if you buy a dress shirt, the salesperson will show you a tie. But the information-based nature of the Amazon system has become a model for many Internet vendors.

The key to point-of-sale information is the ability to use the data to build an effective knowledge-based marketing program. In order to achieve that objective, we need to make the data easy to collect, consistent from customer to customer, and relatively easy to categorize so we can discover insights and trends. Sales and service people need to have a short script of very limited, targeted questions to ask. For example, ask customers, "Why did you buy? Price?" or "How will you use this product?" and then record their responses. This data then needs to go into a database that can be searched for use in designing and promoting products and services.

Customer Surveys

A more common and formal method for acquiring customer information is the survey. Whether in writing, by telephone, or via the Internet, many customers will take the time to provide a company with valuable information about their purchase process, their use of a product or service, their opinions about the product or service, and other relevant information (like demographics, purchase outlet, and measures of satisfaction). Surveys usually take place after a purchase, but it's important to capture the information within a relatively short time. In this fashion, the experiences are fresh in their minds and their interest in the product or service is high. Of course, monitoring customers' views on a long-term basis also can be valuable as a marketing tool. Using the longer-term view, we can spot trends, competitor advances or declines, and additional opportunities.

Surveys should be easy for customers. Do everything you can to let them know that you want their information and that you value their input. In the end, though, people tend to respond better to easy and short survey formats. Usually the best way to do this is to anticipate their answers to questions and provide answer choices. Here's an example:

Which three product features are most important to you?
- Price
- Ease of Use
- Brand
- Ease of Installation
- Ease of Assembly
- Smell
- Color Selections
- Durability
- Other

By asking the respondents to select the three most important answers, you're forcing them to think and prioritize among the choices, an important principle in securing valid data.

Get Help from a Professional

Survey design and administration is a science. While the company seeking the data must determine the content of the survey, it's a good idea to outsource preparation and administration, unless the company has seasoned market research professionals. At the very least, the company should seek consultation on the survey design to ensure that the data will be valid, reliable, and collected efficiently.

Thus, when the data is pooled, you'll have better information for decisions on modifying the product or service, promoting it, and targeting the market. Also you should always offer the opportunity to add information that you may not have anticipated ("Other").

Service organizations should be interested in surveying customers on a regular basis. Take an insurance company, for example. One of the important factors in buying behavior is the insurer's reputation for fast and fair claim service. By monitoring the customer satisfaction with claims services with a survey on each claim, the company can bolster or improve its reputation by adjusting its performance and touting its record of satisfied customers.

J.D. Power

J.D. Power and Associates is a company that specializes in collecting customer-based information through surveying techniques. The company was founded in 1968 and has evolved as a powerful brand in providing unbiased information for customers and companies. Its rankings of products and services are now seen as a standard for product quality and customer satisfaction in a large number of industries. Achieving a J.D. Power top ranking immediately boosts the credibility of a company's marketing information and makes it difficult for competitors to attack these products and services. Additionally, Power can provide a comprehensive set of customer information to companies, in order to determine where products and competitors are weak or strong.

For most companies, surveys are an important part of gathering customer information. Surveys also can provide the most scientifically accurate results regarding all sorts of customer attitudes and behaviors.

Focus Groups

A tool commonly used to gather customer information is the focus group. Focus groups are gatherings of a small group of customers (or non-buyers) led by a trained facilitator, designed to go further in depth regarding customer and non-customer purchase and use information and behaviors. Focus groups, unlike surveys, do not provide statistically valid results *per se,* but rather give us real insights into the buyer's thinking and actions. Use of these groups is very common in consumer products marketing and promotion.

Focus group A professionally moderated discussion within a group of individuals (four or more) whose opinions are thought to represent the target market. The moderator normally guides the discussion, following guidelines or a script drawn up in collaboration with the company.

Focus groups are good for understanding what customers want and how they react to a product or service. The information gained from a focus group is qualitative, rather than quantitative, so they are not as good as surveys for assessing reactions and opinions.

Getting the Most out of Focus Groups

What makes a good and productive focus group? Dr. Phillip E. Downs, President of Kerr & Downs Research in Tallahassee, Florida, a firm that specializes in consumer analysis, says that there are four key elements to getting great results from a focus group.

1. **The Group:** It should consist of eight to 10 participants from a similar target market. There should be no "experts" in the group to dominate the discussion. Usually you need to pay the participants an incentive.

2. **The Moderator:** The moderator is the most important resource in determining the outcome. He or she should be independent, experienced in running focus groups, and knowledgeable about the client and markets. The moderator should be proficient at using tools and exercises to stimulate creativity and discussion.

3. **The Client:** The client should take an active role in generating questions and the script and should be there to unobtrusively observe the group. The client needs to debrief with the moderator soon after the dismissal of the group.

4. **The Facility and Recruiting:** Most groups are taped using hidden cameras. Participants and moderator should be comfortable and at ease in the setting. It's critical to secure the right participants. A strong recruiting script is needed and participants need to be reminded about their appointment with the group to ensure attendance.

More information about focus groups and customer analysis can be found at www.kerr-downs.com.

Focus groups, in addition to providing data about the purchase process and usage of products and services, can also be used to test various ideas. A simple example is the taste test, in which companies, like Coca-Cola, ask consumers to compare and report on various product formulations.

Focus groups are also often used to test advertising appeal. Groups watch various advertisements and report on how favorably disposed they are to the product being promoted.

Focus groups, like all of the consumer analysis techniques, provide information from buyers and nonbuyers about the ele-

Focus Groups May Be ... Too Focused

It can be dangerous to bet too heavily on focus groups. Take the hard lesson learned by Coca-Cola.

In the early 1980s, Coca-Cola and Pepsi-Cola were fighting for consumers. Coke held only a 5% market share lead over Pepsi, although it spent $100 million more per year on advertising. Pepsi was promoting taste tests showing that consumers preferred Pepsi to Coke. So, Coke conducted some 200,000 consumer interviews and developed a formula that beat Pepsi in taste tests.

Coca-Cola replaced its formula in April 1985 and introduced New Coke with a big advertising campaign. Almost immediately there was a strong reaction against the new formula and, only a few months later, Coca-Cola brought back the old formula as Classic Coke.

The hard lesson was that taste tests with focus groups are not infallible. Coca-Cola had invested heavily in focus groups to focus on taste, but it had not considered emotional attachment to the brand.

ments of our strategy, which may include product features, brand, or pricing options. By getting real data from real people, decision makers can test and revise their assumptions about how and why people buy our goods and services.

The key to being successful at gathering and using customer information is to be disciplined and systematic about capturing the data. First, determine what pieces of information are the most valuable to you. Don't load up your wish list. Rather, prioritize the most relevant and important information that's necessary to improve your performance and strategy. Second, select the best forum for getting the information. Getting a few data items from many customers is usually better than getting a lot of data from a few customers. Finally, put the information to work. When customer information differs from assumptions, managers tend to believe their assumptions rather than the data. You will find resistance to changing the business model, strategy, or even operational issues. Try to validate the information and take action to change approaches to meet customer demands. We know that the customer is always right!

Can We Meet the Needs of Those Buying from Competitors, Without Sacrificing Value to Our Customers?

OK, so we don't have 100% market share and never will. But how do we get more of the business that's going to our competitors—without losing the bird in the hand (our current customers) to gain the bird in the bush (those buying from competitors). How do we figure this out?

The first step we've taken already: we must collect the customer data and analyze it. The second step is to formulate a competitive strategy. We'll discuss developing competitive strategy a little later on; for now we'll look at some of the levers that we have to work with to adjust our performance in competitive markets.

We need to modify our *marketing mix*—the combination of product, place, promotion, and price that we're offering to a target segment. Almost everyone who's studied marketing has heard of the four P's: these are the tools that we can use to move customers from competitors' products to our products.

Within each of the P's of the marketing mix, there are many component factors with which to work. Remember that we want to use the data that we have on our consumers and nonbuyers to determine how to grow best. Let's consider each one.

Marketing mix The combination of product, place, promotion, and price that a company offers to target customers. The term became popular in marketing circles after Neil H. Borden published an article, "The Concept of the Marketing Mix," in 1965. Since then, others have added P's to the marketing mix: *people, physical evidence* (such as facilities, Web sites, and uniforms), *process* (the whole customer experience), and *prospect* (potential customers).

> ### Don't Assume Customer Loyalty
> Schlitz beer of Milwaukee was number two in sales to
> Budweiser nationally for years. Managers at Schlitz
> decided to go after share and also increase profits through reducing
> costs. They chose to change the formulation of their beer to use less
> expensive ingredients and use the savings to spend more on advertis-
> ing to attack Bud. But they forgot one thing: their customers liked the
> taste of the beer and did not like the taste of the new Schlitz formula.
> The result was disastrous for the brand and the company. Not only
> did they not beat Bud, but they continually lost share, and today the
> brand is virtually extinct. The moral of the tale is not to take your cus-
> tomers for granted when changing product features and options.

Product

One choice that we have to gain more market share is to modify
the product in some way. The obvious first consideration is features and options. Since we know something about the tastes and
preferences of buyers and nonbuyers, there may be some adjustments that will retain our current customers, but attract some of
those people who have been buying from our competitors.

When we have information that quality (or perceived quality)
is an issue, then we might choose to improve product quality to
garner more share. Of course, quality comes neither easily nor
cheaply. Related to quality is the warranty offered. Warranties
can be used to modify attitudes toward perceived lower quality.

Other product adjustments that we can evaluate are brand,
packaging, product line, and service issues. In each case, information provided to us will shape the best options to increase
our share against the competition.

Place

"Place" refers to the physical and marketing space associated
with buying the product. Therefore, it includes the distribution
channel, the store location, and any logistics issues (like inventory or transportation).

Establishing Quality Reputation Through Warranties

Hyundai Motor Company of Korea had little name recognition when it entered the U.S. market in 1986. Furthermore, its products clustered in the low-price, entry-level segment of the market. Hyundai's perceived quality was uncertain at best. To counter the uncertainty, Hyundai offered the longest (10 years/100,000 miles) and most generous warranty in the car business. This warranty led potential car buyers to give Hyundai a try and many bought. Over time Hyundai has gained a stronger and stronger foothold in the U.S. market.

One reason we may not be reaching more customers is because of our distribution choices. Insurance companies, for example, can use independent agents (representing more than one company), exclusive agents, or direct selling (via the Internet, telephone, or mail). Some customer segments may prefer one channel or another, so we lose business to those competitors that use a preferred channel. This reasoning is behind a big trend in insurance and many other businesses to a multi-channel approach, using more than one distribution option.

Promotion

Advertising, sales techniques, and publicity all contribute to the marketing mix as promotions. Advertising and promotions of all kinds communicate the value of a product or service to buyers across all aspects of the marketing mix. For example, when an airline runs a sale during a fare war, you frequently see or hear a tag line, "Contact ABC Airlines or your travel agent." The ad promotes not only the low price, but also the multiple channels (the travel agent, an 800 number, or the Web site) through which you can buy tickets.

Ads can be very influential at attracting market share from competitors, communicating information to competitors' customers that changes their buying considerations. Ads can also promote a brand concept. For example, Ritz-Carlton Hotel ads basically show people being served as they relax in luxury. The Ritz-Carlton brand stands for luxury, service, and a serene environment in which to unwind.

> ## Knowledge Pays Off
> **Smart Managing**
>
> Companies and their people can use various methods for garnering attention and positive share results via the free media (newspapers, radio, television). One way is to get corporate leaders and technicians listed as experts for the media to call on breaking news. Stories in the paper or on the radio or TV about government policy or economic conditions, for example, will often include quotes by local personalities. This attention positions the people and their organizations as leaders and can provide name and brand recognition that will increase sales. All it takes is someone to volunteer to be an expert on some appropriate topic and get onto the media outlets' lists.

Price

The last of the four P's is price. For most companies, price is the last consideration for finding additional growth, but maybe the most critical. The components of price are level, discounts, and payment terms. As a company competes, managers keep their fingers on the pulse of pricing, because price is where the buyer determines the value equation. Buyers will compare the prices-features ratio among various alternatives and judge whether differences among the offerings are worth the price differentials.

Store brands, often called private labels, provide an interesting look at buyer behavior in price comparisons. Store brands, like Walgreens, Albertson's, and other retailers, essentially copy the features, packaging, and quality of name-brand goods, but offer products at a significantly lower price level.

Name brands often compete through pricing adjustments, like offering coupons or other in-store promotions. Name brands also introduce product improvements and innovations, quickly followed by the private labelers. Store-brand manufacturers need to be fast followers, while name-brand makers need to invest in research and product development. Private-label goods put a dent in the name-brand sales, but often name-brand manufacturers are actually producing the private-label goods. By producing goods under their name brand and under private labels, the manufacturers protect their market share or even take share from their competitors.

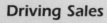

Driving Sales

As the price of new cars has risen and the availability of quality, low-mileage used cars has increased, auto companies have resorted to using discounting and payment terms as the principal means of stimulating demand. Cash rebates and zero or very low interest on financing have become two of the dominant means of competing in the car business. Dealers find that having great terms and rebate offers can take pressure off negotiations around the purchase price.

If we work the marketing mix, we can attempt to attract customers away from or competitors to our products or services. One tool we can use to explore the dynamics of the competitive marketplace for our goods is called the *product-positioning map.*

Here's how we use this tool. Let's take as our example the market for sport utility vehicles— SUVs, the rage of the car-buying world.

We first identify two critical factors by which customers differentiate among products in the market. Suppose we learn from our customers and noncustomers that two of the most important factors are capacity (room for people and "stuff") and mileage (particularly as gas prices rise).

Then, we create a quadrant, labeling the extremes of the X axis "small capacity" and "large capacity" and the extremes of the Y axis "low gas mileage" and "high gas mileage." We place on this quadrant the competing products and our

Product-Positioning Map

A product-positioning map is a graphic representation of a product according to two criteria that drive the purchase of that product. The map allows an organization to determine where one of its products stands in the minds of consumers and in comparison with competing products.

To create a positioning map, you first identify two criteria, such as quality and price or convenience and flavor. Then you create a quadrant with one criterion serving as the X axis and the other serving as the Y axis; label the extremes of each axis to indicate high and low. Next, position your product relative to the two criteria; do the same with each of the competing products.

product. This shows us how our product compares with competing products on these two criteria. By overlaying the market share or sales units, we can see what people are buying.

Figure 4-1 shows an SUV product-positioning map based on these two factors. Each point represents a product; the size of the point reflects the unit sales volume for each product. The map indicates that capacity and mileage are inversely related; that is, as capacity increases, mileage decreases. This map also shows that dominant sales are of medium- to large-capacity SUVs with moderate gas mileage. This map suggests that, as gas mileage becomes more important, a company that can engineer an SUV with large capacity and high mileage would attract customers. On the other hand, products A and B on the map may simply try to gain competitive sales by promoting their products in new ways. Product A might emphasize that it has the best mileage in its size class to try to take share from both smaller SUVs and large models with much lower mileage.

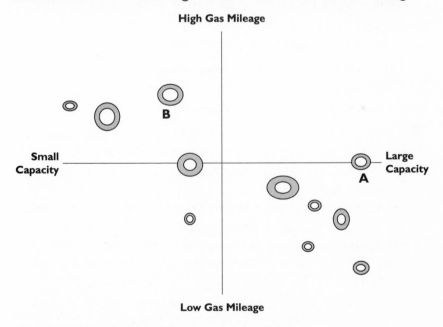

Figure 4-1. Product positioning map for SUVs

Product B may be able to take share from all SUVs as the SUV with the best gas mileage, period.

Product–positioning maps provide a nice visual of the marketplace and, although they can capture only two dimensions, these are useful tools. In particular, they can help us determine how to use customer information, to take business from competitors.

What Else Can We Do for Our Customers to Create Value for Them and for Ourselves?

If we learn how to satisfy our customers better, oftentimes we will sell more and, importantly, usually our profitability will increase. A widely held research finding is that repeat customers are more profitable than new customers because the costs of selling to current buyers are lower. How do we do that?

One way is by analyzing the entire buyer experience in detail. Customers interact with our company in many ways; by examining each of these interactions, we can find more ways to add value. These are the common buyer interactions, which you'll remember from Chapter 1 as the six phases of a purchase:

- purchase
- delivery
- use
- supplements
- maintenance
- disposal

A format for looking at the potential for improving the buyer experience at each step is to map important buyer factors, learned through gathering information from customers, for each of the interactions.

Suppose, for example, the two most important reasons for buying from our company are convenience and image (or brand). Using this approach, we determine how we might add value by focusing on these two factors at all stages of the customer experience. If convenience and image are important to the sale, then we should explore how we could satisfy convenience and image demands in delivery, use, supplements, maintenance, and disposal as well.

Leader of the Pack

The Harley-Davidson brand is one of the strongest in the U.S. Harley sells motorcycles. But Harley has created quite a large additional business by using the brand in its supplements, including clothes, motorcycle supplies, and accessories.

In 2001, Harley-Davidson licensed its brand to Ford to provide a Harley-Davidson F-150 pickup truck to match buyers' needs and brand loyalty with "a little bit of attitude and a lot of personality." Then, for its 100th anniversary in 2003, it licensed its brand to Motorola, which offered cell phones customized in black with leather or chrome and engraved with the Harley-Davidson 100th anniversary logo.

If convenience is important to a buyer's decision to purchase, then it seems reasonable that convenient delivery and maintenance might also be valued highly. If brand is important, maybe we can bring brand to maintenance. General Motors has done just that with the Mr. Goodwrench approach to branding maintenance, first within dealerships and, more recently, in freestanding GM Goodwrench service centers.

Even in disposal we can find new ways to satisfy customers. As mentioned earlier, Nevada Bob's golf store created a market for used clubs, which was a barrier to new sales. That is, as shoppers looked at new equipment, they wondered what would they do with their old clubs. By taking used clubs in trade for the new purchase, the store made it easier for shoppers to buy new clubs.

Use Green to Make Green

Disposal is often an interaction that companies do not analyze deeply. The environment is an important social issue and can be a differentiator for vendors. By finding environmentally friendly ways to dispose of products, some companies can be more attractive to current customers and draw new ones. For example, Office Depot promotes the disposal of printer, fax, and copier cartridges in an environmentally sensitive fashion through in-store depositories. Of course, trips to Office Depot to drop off cartridges mean traffic for the stores and potentially additional sales.

Throughout this chapter we have explored the necessity and methods for doing comprehensive, systematic, and creative customer analysis. Such an analysis and the information that it provides are essential to operating our business and creating better strategies.

Manager's Checklist for Chapter 4

❏ Analysis of customers and nonbuyers is essential.

❏ Getting good, regular, and valid information from our markets must be a management priority.

❏ We need to know who are customers are and who buys from competitors.

❏ We need to know why our customers buy from us and why some choose to buy from competitors.

❏ Smart companies get out into the marketplace, talk to buyers and nonbuyers alike, train sales and service people to collect data from buyers, and use experts to gather scientific survey data and to conduct focus groups to gain qualitative information.

❏ Successful organizations use their information technology to create more value through adjusting the marketing mix and applying what they know to the entire customer experience.

Internal Business Analysis

Every year only one team wins the NFL Super Bowl, the NBA Title, the Stanley Cup, and the World Series. All of the other teams are left asking, "Why didn't we win?" Then changes are made. Trades are consummated. Draft choices are selected. Coaches and general managers are fired. Training camps focus on weaknesses and deficiencies.

These decisions are made based upon a formal examination of the performance of the entire organization. All aspects of offense and defense are scrutinized. Coaching plans and drills are reviewed critically. The front office examines its processes and decision-making in the administrative areas.

In business, the same rules apply. However, in business we have a chance to win it all with every sale, with every quarter's results, or with the completion of every year. Whether we win or not in these circumstances, taking a good hard look at the numbers and all of the activities that delivered the results is a valuable exercise. If we're embarking upon the task of developing strategy, this kind of internal review is essential.

Internal Audit

Every year most firms hire a CPA firm to conduct an external audit of their financial statements and internal financial controls. This audit follows a formal process and involves virtually all of the financial staff of the organization.

That's not good enough for an internal audit designed to assist in the development of corporate strategy. There are two differences: first, the internal audit is a comprehensive review of all aspects of the business, not just financial results, and second, the internal audit requires the cooperation and inputs of managers and staff from all areas of the business.

The audit process usually involves the leadership of a key executive and a mixed disciplinary team to compile the results. The end result of the process is an intimate understanding of the organization and its processes and, most importantly, an assessment of the strengths and weaknesses in each of the functional areas of the operation. However, an absolute critical result of the audit must be an integrated review of the business. This means that managers must evaluate effectiveness of cross-disciplinary activities and communications. Are the R&D folks effectively communicating to the marketing staff, for example, regarding the new product development schedule? In return, is the marketing and sales team getting the correct competitive information from the marketplace to the R&D staff in order to remain a leader in new product development?

In order to motivate an integrated approach, the audit is not organized by functions, but rather by the components of the business model. There are four components to such a comprehensive internal audit:

- results
- people
- functions and processes
- relationships

Results Audit

The results audit is the easiest piece, for two reasons.

First, the performance review discussed in Chapter 3 really

provides the information necessary to sort out our strengths and weaknesses from a results point of view. In that review, we followed a five-step process to assess the current performance of the critical, key drivers of our business. We used techniques such as gap analysis and benchmarking to identify successes and problem areas.

Second, as we'll see later in the book, implementing strategy also means establishing important metrics for ongoing measurement. The system that we establish in that context will automatically provide the results information that we require.

This is not to say that we should not challenge the available information for its appropriateness, relevance, and accuracy. Our results audit synthesizes information and provides a detailed assessment of the performance of the organization via the metrics employed. We're searching for the strengths and weaknesses of the company and the numbers will lead us there. The end result is a comprehensive measurement of our performance in key areas over time and relative to objectives, competitors, customer expectations, and best practices. The other three audits that we propose are used to explain the performance results found in this step of the analysis.

People Audit

The people audit needs to address the fundamental questions:

- Do we have the right people in the right places?
- Are we prepared for any loss of personnel?
- Can we attract the right people for the future of the company?
- Are our employees satisfied with the work environment?
- Are our people trained and developed to ensure that the company can pursue its values and fulfill its mission?

The first question—right people, right places—is a performance question. As we set new goals and strategy, do we have the capability to get the job done with the people currently in place? In some cases, the answer is clear, one way or the other.

Key Term

Job rotation Programs that shift an employee periodically from one job to another, to provide different experiences and develop skills and knowledge. For functional managers, job rotation programs provide opportunities to gain exposure to management issues in other disciplines. A financial analyst, for example, may be given an assignment on a new product development team in order to gain marketing exposure. Usually the assignments are temporary. The objective is to give functional experts broad experience so that they can move into general and senior management positions.

In others, it's a matter of development, educationally and experientially. In those cases, we need to provide the exposure to executive education programs for the education component and possibly job rotation for broadening experiences.

The second question—Are we prepared for any loss of personnel?—is asking about the succession plan. Managers must be prepared in case a key staff member were to leave the organization because of death, illness, or resignation. A succession plan is simply a list of the employees who would be able to assume a new position, if it became necessary. Some of these individuals may not be ready today because of a lack of experience or training. In other cases, there are no internal successors identified.

CAUTION!

Keep It Confidential
The people audit is not a public audit. And, in fact, the process should be conducted so that only a few key individuals see the overall results. Each manager must present his or her assessment of all subordinates, but the overall strengths, weaknesses, and succession plan results of the people audit need to reside with a select few.

One of the objectives of the people audit is to fully develop a succession plan, all the way to the CEO spot. Of course, CEO successor planning is the task of the Board of Directors. A good succession plan consists of two steps:

• Inventory possible replacements in terms of potential, skills, and gaps.

> **Keep a Picture of the Succession Plan**
> One way to get a handle on how prepared the organization is for any personnel losses is to take an organization chart and list the potential successors for each key position. Next to each name, estimate how many months it will take for the person to be ready for the job. If it requires more than 36 months, the person is probably not ready to be a successor. If there are no names available, circle that job in red. For those jobs, start preparing now for whatever might happen: find the right recruiter, execute an employment contract, and identify potential successors outside the organization.

- Outline a development plan for each possible replacement and incorporate it into the performance management process for him or her.

The third question is about attracting the right people for the future of the company. When we find a weakness, we must remedy it; sometimes that means replacing someone who isn't fully capable of doing the job. When we find an opportunity, we should find people to help make the most of it. But what if we couldn't recruit anyone qualified? Not because there were not any qualified applicants, but because none would be willing to accept a position at our firm.

The people audit provides the organization an opportunity to look carefully at its ability to recruit the talent that it needs to succeed. The human resources system should track the results of past recruiting efforts and competitive salary and benefits levels. Just as we can learn from customers who buy from our competitors, we can learn from candidates who choose not to take our offer of employment.

The people audit also needs to be broader than the management of the company. On a regular cycle, most companies hire outside consultants to conduct employee attitude surveys. The people audit needs to use the information in those reports to assess the current work environment in the company, to answer the fourth question on our list—Are our employees satisfied with the work environment?

Smart Managing

Satisfaction Sells

Just as we can use customer satisfaction evaluations or a high J.D. Power rating to help sell our products or services, we can use broad employee satisfaction results to sell the firm to candidates. It's most impressive to potential new employees to see an improving work environment and a satisfied group of potential coworkers. Carefully using the results of employee attitude surveys can be helpful as a way to market your company as an employer, both with current employees and with candidates.

The final question in the people audit deals with training and human development. Are our people trained and developed to ensure that the company can pursue its values and fulfill its mission? In other words, how well do we support our people in their quest to grow as individuals and employees? In *Fortune*'s annual report on the best companies to work for, look at the investment in training that the top companies provide to their people.

It's Not About Time or Money

Although quantitative measures of training (hours and dollars) may be useful for comparisons, they should definitely not be the basis of any training initiatives. For one reason, quantitative measures are inadequate when your goal is qualitative. For another, a lot of valuable training is on the job and/or just in time, so it's harder to measure in terms of time and money. So, track the hours and dollars to determine the cost of training, but definitely not to evaluate the results!

Training hours is one of the key factors in determining the top companies and employees respond well to quality training and executive development programs.

Of course, the organization benefits greatly by being a company that supports the growth and development of its staff. In addition to building satisfaction, attracting better candidates, and retaining employees better, companies that are strong in development benefit from increased expertise, innovation, and profitability.

Functions and Processes Audit

Every business can be organized in a value chain framework. Whether we're delivering pizza in the suburbs, providing finan-cial services on Wall Street, or making airplane engines for the world market, the business can be modeled as a chain of processes from ideas, to assets, to income. The generic busi-ness value chain is depicted in Figure 5-1.

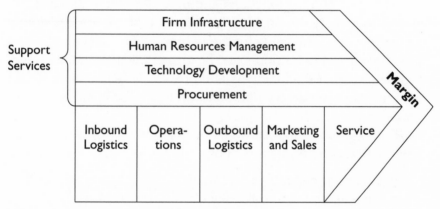

Figure 5-1. Generic value chain model

Businesses are divided into two components: support serv-ices and primary activities. Note that a key emphasis of using the value chain model is to show that *all* areas of the company can contribute to profit margins, if they deliver value along the way. Support services include administration and overhead (infrastructure), human resources, technology, and procure-ment. Primary activities include inbound logistics, operations, outbound logistics, marketing and sales, and service.

To give the value chain some reality, let's look at it for Coors Brewing. What are the primary activities? "Inbound logistics" refers to acquiring the materials to make beer—water, hops, cereal grains (rice and refined corn starches), and barley—and the equipment necessary for brewing. "Operations" refers to the processes by which the ingredients are turned into beer: the manufacturing and bottling or canning. "Outbound logistics" refers to getting the product to the distribution network, typically beer wholesalers. "Marketing and sales" refers to those activities associated with getting Coors beer onto the shelves of liquor and grocery stores, into taverns, to vendors at ball games, and, finally, into the hands of beer drinkers. "Service" refers to the activities of ensuring that consumers, retailers, and wholesalers of Coors beer are happy with the experience of working with the company and enjoying its product.

In conducting the functions and processes audit, the first step is to identify the principal processes that are the key drivers in delivering the value for the company. The important processes need to be prioritized first, then audited and analyzed. Ultimately, all of the functions and processes will be audited, but it's important to be very rigorous with the most significant processes first.

For example, suppose we determine the following most critical functions and processes in our company:

- access to capital
- supplier cost and reliability
- manufacturing flexibility

The audit would then look at these areas for strengths and weaknesses in a critical and detailed way.

Access to capital is very important for firms with capital-intensive expansion plans, for example. The audit would examine the company's credit rating and debt capacity to determine both the availability of debt and the costs of borrowing. The company would look to its existing covenants to determine the extent of flexibility it has in securing additional levels of debt. The audit would investigate how possible, easy, and expensive raising new equity capital is for the company. Finally, the investigation would explore the history of the company in generating the additional cash flows from expansion to determine the coverage of the debt costs, or the returns to equity holders if these capital sources were tapped.

Some companies might identify their suppliers' cost and reliability as a key resource. Looking at the processes by which the

---

ButterBurgers® Spreading

In Chapter 2 we discussed Culver's, the custard and fast food chain based in Wisconsin that has grown to 200 stores in a relatively short time. In order to build outlets at that pace, Culver's needs access to capital to buy land and build stores. Culver's also needs to know what the ramp-up period for cash flows is for a new store, so they can determine at what point in its life a new store will begin to fully be able to pay for its capital costs. In order to implement aggressive growth strategies, companies like Culver's need access to capital and a well-planned process for expansion. For more information about Culver's growth and frachise system, see *Forbes* magazine, June 9, 2003, p. 135.

---

business acquires its input materials then becomes an important part of the audit. For some companies, the price of raw materials is the absolute key to determining their profitability. For example, if our company produces plastic packaging or wrap, the price of polyvinyl chloride (PVC) resin pellets is an important driver to our business's success. The audit would look at our process and evaluate the expertise and effectiveness of the procurement department. In some cases, like PVC, we can hedge prices through futures contracts; in others, we might negotiate harder with suppliers or form a buying group to gain more power for better pricing. The audit does not necessarily draw us to a conclusion about changing the process, but rather evaluates results to determine if changes are warranted.

If we prioritized that manufacturing flexibility is a key driver to our business model, the audit would examine lead-time performance and buyer satisfaction results, among others. In some cases, manufacturing operations need to be able to change a manufacturing line quickly to accommodate customer needs and demands. For example, private label manufacturers typically need to have this capability. When a good customer runs out of stock and demands quick delivery of goods, the manufacturer may have to stop the line, interrupt the current job, change the dies or packaging, and run the new job. By having the flexibility to change over quickly, the manufacturer meets the customers' needs. The audit will not only consider the frequency and impact of job interruptions, but also will investigate the causes. If, for example, the manufacturer had better inventory information or knew when store promotions were occurring, it might be able to reduce the incidence of job interruptions. The audit might expose the weaknesses in our customer information systems that lead to these costly line changeovers.

The point of these examples is to reveal how we might approach an audit of our functions and processes. First, we must identify and rank the important areas to audit. Second, we must thoughtfully detail the results of key metrics in the processes and identify our strengths and weaknesses. At the end of our audit, we should know more about our current performance and our capabilities or incapabilities so that we can better understand our organization's potential. The audit should be honest, critical, and motivating for the company to improve the functions or the processes.

Relationships Audit

Remember our general business model: ideas-assets-income. And assets means people, property, and relationships. The relationships audit evaluates critically the important relationships that we might have in our corporate life. Important relationships vary from firm to firm, but any external entity can breed an important relationship. A labor union may be the most important relationship in some companies, such as an airline. A government regulator may be all-important in another corporation, such as a public utility. The distribution network may be the most vital for an insurance company.

The audit begins by identifying all of the relationships that are important in order for the company to succeed. Then this list needs to be rank-ordered by importance.

Once we know the most important item on the list, we begin to evaluate that relationship in detail. We look to the key drivers of the relationship and the levers of influence that can be applied to change the dynamics of the interaction.

A Hospital Relationship in the ICU

A well-known children's hospital was experiencing very poor results, for its finances and its reputation. Morale was poor among the staff and occupancy levels were trending down. The hospital formed a task force to investigate the situation. The result of its report was simply refocusing on its value chain and a key relationship.

A children's hospital must rely upon physicians from a broad catchment area to refer their child patients. Those patients can be admitted to their local general hospitals, so a children's hospital must provide reasons for physicians to send their child·patients out of their care and away from their local hospital.

But the task force found that the children's hospital had not created a strong relationship with referring physicians. Indeed, communications were poor and follow-up was spotty. Although the care delivered was good, referring physicians did not feel good about it. The task force's job became a relationship audit for referring physicians and the children's hospital began to understand (again) that this relationship was vital to its success. As a result, the hospital put a lot of energy into reaching out and improving the process—with amazingly good results.

SWOT Analysis

The culmination of the activities that have been described—the current performance review, the scanning of the external environment, the customer analysis, the internal audit—is the SWOT analysis. This analysis, as defined and briefly outlined in Chapter 3, focuses on strengths, weaknesses, opportunities, and threats. The SWOT analysis is the principal input into the strategy development process. Whether we use a sophisticated strategic development process or a simple one, SWOT provides the foundation for finding the strategic direction for our firm.

SWOT analysis itself is relatively easy, if we've done all the prep work outlined in the strategic development process. It's a matter of synthesizing all the information and integrating customer, environmental, and internal assessment data into a useable package for making decisions. This information will be used to determine the feasibility of strategic alternatives, once they've been identified. Importantly, we can also match our external and internal findings to create powerful strategies for the future success of the company.

The organization of information is absolutely critical in this matter. The goal is to report a list of the five to 10 best strengths of the company, the five to 10 most important weaknesses, the five to 10 best opportunities for the company, and the five to 10 most critical threats to our success and potentially our survival.

Strengths

Strengths can be internal or external. For example, we may have strength in our financing because our cost of capital is extremely low. That strength is internal. Alternatively, we may be operating in a growth market, say pharmaceuticals for the elderly. That strength is external.

Before you put an item on the list of strengths, you must assess the facts. For example, many companies believe that their brand is strong. Believing is not enough. If we're potentially going to bet our future on the brand, we need to verify, through market research and customer data, that indeed the brand carries weight in the marketplace. We also need to know which segments of the market would rate our brand favorably. Finally, we must know what our brand conveys to the market. Applying the brand inappropriately, even if the brand is strong, can be very detrimental.

Cadillac Goes Small

The Cadillac brand has long stood for large, luxury cars. When many other companies were doing very well with mid-sized luxury cars (BMW, Lexus, Mercedes), Cadillac decided to enter the mid-sized market in 1997 with the Catera. While the car had many Cadillac signature features, its size and appointments did not match with either traditional Cadillac buyers or competitors. The car was discontinued after the 2001 model.

Contrast this experience with the Escalade, an SUV and truck line now being produced by Cadillac. Even though the brand was brought to a totally new segment, the size and stature of the vehicles were consistent with the brand and these vehicles have done extremely well.

To establish the working list of strengths, I suggest that each of the previous analyses be explored and the top three strengths of each be noted. The previous analysis projects include:

- Current Performance Review
  - Results compared with goals
  - Results compared with history
  - Results compared with competitors
  - Results compared with benchmarks
  - Results compared with customer expectations
- Environmental Analysis
  - Social factors and trends
  - Economic factors and trends
  - Political/regulatory factors and trends
  - Technology factors and trends
- Industry Analysis
  - Structure and size
  - Competition
- Customer Analysis
  - Who are our customers?
  - Why do they buy from us?
  - Who buys from the competitors and why?
  - Are they satisfied and, if so, why?
- Internal Audit
  - Results
  - People
  - Functions and processes
  - Relationships

Ask the team to choose the three best strengths that flow from each of these categories. Then collect all of them on a list, remove those that are marginal, and pick the ones that a consensus believes are the true strengths of the company. When you do this in a group, each strength that makes the final list will have to be justified with facts and data to prove the point. Limit the final number to five, or certainly no more than 10 items. It will be tough, but the final set will be strong!

Weaknesses

Start the whole process again, but this time we're looking for trouble, the weak spots. Again, weaknesses can be internal or external. For example, we may determine that our R&D efforts and program are weak. That weakness is internal. But we may also find, for instance, that technology trends mean a softer market for our traditional goods, so our market is getting smaller. That weakness is external.

In the analysis of weaknesses, we need to consider two perspectives. The first is the view from inside the company. Do we consider it a weakness? The second important perspective is from the competitors. What do they consider our weaknesses? As we'll see, competitors may attack what they consider as weaknesses in the market. So it's important for us to know both perspectives.

We make a list of the top three weaknesses from each category, also looking for factors that may appear as weaknesses to our competitors. We then distill the list to five to 10 items and single out a few as targets for competitors.

Northwest Pursues Midwest

The post-September 11 market conditions for airlines have been very difficult. Terrorism and airport security inconveniences have made passengers stay at home or take other modes of transportation. At the same time, fuel prices have soared as the Middle East remains in conflict. With the notable exception of Southwest Airlines and the new JetBlue Airways, most carriers have done poorly, in varying degrees.

Midwest Airlines (formerly Midwest Express, based in Milwaukee) has been hit hard by these troubles and is in financial trouble. Seeing the financial weakness at Midwest, Northwest Airlines (based in Minneapolis) invested in new, direct service routes flying from Milwaukee to New York, Los Angeles, Phoenix, DC, and Boston—Midwest's best routes. Northwest saw a weakness at Midwest and is trying to exploit the opportunity. That's hardball!

Turn the Table

One way to see what the competitor sees is to become the competitor. Here's a simple tool to help you do that. Figure 5-2 is a vulnerability chart. We list the key elements of the value chain on the left. Then we pretend to be competitors.

	Vulnerable?	Weakness	Potential	How?
R&D				
Quality				
Operations				
Marketing				
Sales				
Service				
Finance				
HR				

Figure 5-2. Vulnerability chart

We ask, "Is this piece of the value chain vulnerable?" If the answer is no, because the area is a strength, move on. If, however, the response is yes, then we ask more questions.

Next we ask, "What is the weakness?" Here we want to be specific with our answers. For example, the weakness in R&D might be the long time it takes for products to leave the R&D area or the sales weakness may be the lack of experienced salespeople beyond one or two "stars."

Competitors would then rank the potential of each weak area in terms of whether it can further their objectives significantly. For those vulnerabilities that have good potential, the competitors would then draw up a plan of attack. In the R&D case, they might come to market with successive, quick product improvements and take customers. In the case of the salespeople, they may steal the "stars" and leave just the inexperienced staff.

Opportunities

Many authors on this topic think that opportunities arise only from the external environment. I disagree. Opportunities for growth and profit can be found in the external factors and trends, of course, but also from exploring internal activities as well. For example, unused space may be capable of generating revenue by leasing it to vendors. That's an internally driven opportunity. In fact, one of three key methods used in this book to identify strategic opportunities focuses on asset utilization, that is, making the most of the assets that we own. This is a totally internal perspective for finding strategic thrusts.

External opportunities are significant as well. The Hispanic population of the U.S. has grown from 22.4 million in 1990 to 35.3 million in 2000, a growth rate of 58%. Compare that growth with the overall U.S. population growth of only 13.2% during the same period. What companies benefited from this opportunity? Probably none better than Wal-Mart, which recognized that Hispanic populations were more concentrated (75% of Hispanics live in the West and Southwest) and located stores near their communities. Wal-Mart also caters to Hispanic patrons with bilingual signage, staff, and advertising.

Looking at population trends is the classic way to look for opportunities. But opportunities also arise in economic conditions, regulatory changes, and all of the other analyses that we've completed for our company.

Not surprisingly, I recommend that we follow the same procedure to identify new opportunities as we've used for strengths and weaknesses. We find the three best opportunities from each segment of the analysis and whittle the list down to five to 10 overall.

Whittling the list down is the difficulty for the opportunities, because it requires that we assess the strength of the opportunities without a comprehensive discounted cash flow (DCF) analysis. Without doing DCF, we might discard some very valuable opportunities. To minimize the risk of lost opportunities, it's important to have a team with members experienced in all business disciplines (including production, marketing, and finance) pare the list. Opportunities should be ranked with some kind of attractiveness score that correlates with the concepts of DCF, even if the estimates are very rough.

Threats

Look at what's happening to restaurants and hardware stores in the U.S. The trends are scary if you own such a business. Independent restaurants are threatened by fast food outlets and by sit-down chain restaurants (Applebee's, Outback Steakhouse, Macaroni Grill, P.F. Chang's China Bistro). If you run an Ace or a True Value hardware store, it's much the same situation. Watch out for Lowe's and Home Depot. These are real business threats in today's marketplace.

Do you want more worries? Look to China. The Chinese are promoting that they can make anything. Give them a template and the product will be out in short order. Even Mexico is losing manufacturing business to China. Why? Because cost is exceptional and quality is OK. I was surprised to see a piece of Drexel Heritage furniture, an old-line North Carolina furniture company, be delivered in a box marked "made in China." Of course, on the flip side, China is a tremendous cost-saving and market opportunity, if the markets open up and incomes can sustain imported goods.

> **Take Threats Seriously** /!\ CAUTION! /!\
>
> Arthur Andersen was the world's biggest and possibly most respected accounting firm. In a span of less than two years, the firm essentially disappeared off the face of the earth. This startling fact is a reminder that threats to our business, any business, can be disastrous.

Putting the SWOT Analysis Together

At the end of the task, we should have a list of five to 10 good, solid entries in each of the SWOT categories. If we construct a matrix like that in Figure 5-3, we can fine-tune strategic development by exploring various combinations of the identified items, in a slightly more sophisticated fashion than just "seize opportunities" and "shore up weaknesses."

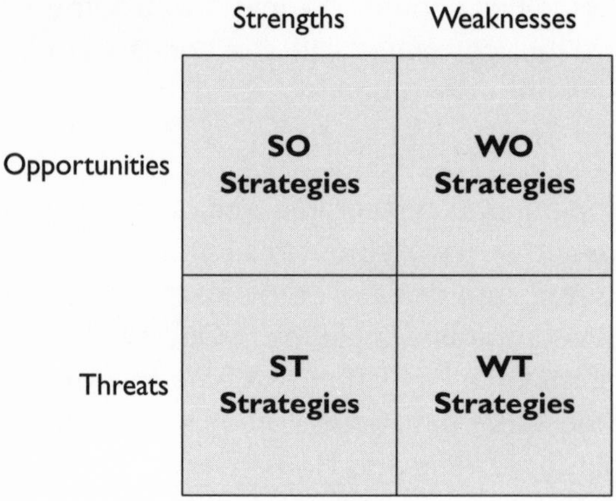

	Strengths	Weaknesses
Opportunities	**SO** Strategies	**WO** Strategies
Threats	**ST** Strategies	**WT** Strategies

Figure 5-3. SWOT strategy map

This approach is relatively straightforward. We match the various findings to make strategy options. There are four categories:

- **SO Strategies**—use our strengths to take advantage of an opportunity.
- **ST Strategies**—use our strengths to minimize a threat.
- **WO Strategies**—improve weaknesses through an opportunity.
- **WT Strategies**—evaluate weaknesses in light of realistic threats.

In each grouping we may find one or two potential strategies, because not all of the possibilities will line up well. Here are a few examples:

- **SO Strategy**—The Disney Company's strength via movies and television allows it to market products and services to baby boomers, their children, and their grandchildren.
- **ST Strategy**—Microsoft's programming strength creates Office Suite, crushing the leading individual vendors of word processing (WordPerfect), data bases (DB2), spreadsheets (Lotus), and presentation software (Harvard Graphics).

- **WO Strategy**—Anthem (a publicly traded collection of Blue Cross health insurance companies) saw the opportunity to convert and merge Blue Cross plans that addressed its weakness, the inability to raise capital to fund growth.
- **WT Strategy**—United Airlines moves to bankruptcy due to financial weakness as it renegotiates its union contracts for concessions and gains government subsidies while facing multiple threats from post-September 11 issues.

By matching positions of strength or weakness with opportunities and threats, we can see potential for new business ideas that will help us meet our goals. This is just a beginning and a taste of strategic alternatives development. Much more will be presented later in the book.

Manager's Checklist for Chapter 5

❑ A careful internal audit is a necessary prerequisite to strategy formulation.

❑ The internal audit should explore operational and financial results, evaluate the company's talent pool, assess the functions and processes, and explore the health of its important relationships.

❑ While most of the internal audit can be done with interdisciplinary teams, the people audit requires more confidentiality and limiting distribution of the findings.

❑ A good SWOT analysis not only identifies the component strengths, weaknesses, opportunities, and threats, but also prioritizes them and limits analysis to a small set of the most important factors.

❑ The SWOT analysis can be used to begin the strategy formulation process by matching strengths and weaknesses against opportunities and threats.

Strategic Choices

Look at three businesses with target markets and goals that appear to be similar: Wal-Mart, Kmart, and Target. Do these firms buy, market, merchandise, promote, and operate differently? Are their results different? Clearly the answer to both questions is yes.

These companies, while in similar businesses, have different strategies. All three companies sell a broad scope of retail goods and position themselves as discounters. All three companies build stores nationally. But the similarities end there.

Wal-Mart is relentless in the pursuit of low prices. Wal-Mart hammers its suppliers, limits overhead, and, as a result, has grown to be the nation's largest retailer. Target focuses its appeal to women and, while prices are discounted, the emphasis is on store appearance, merchandising, and layout. Target's success is linked to customer satisfaction and loyalty. Kmart's strategy is less clear. In many ways, Kmart attempted to mimic the Wal-Mart low price strategy, but did not follow through as aggressively as Wal-Mart in managing costs. Kmart also adopted a branding strategy, like using Martha Stewart, in parts of its operation, which in some ways conflicts with the low-price approach. Kmart's results have been dismal: the firm has declared bankruptcy, reorganized, and closed many stores.

Strategic choices matter. Choices that are adopted must then be implemented in a way that consistently supports the strategic approach of the company throughout its operations.

Generic Strategies

One of the most powerful and easiest ways to delineate strategies was developed by Michael Porter of Harvard Business School. Porter suggests that there are really only three strategies available to business, which he dubbed *generic strategies*:

- low-cost producer
- industry-wide differentiation
- niche player

Low-Cost Producer Strategy

For the most part, cost leadership is a strategy that entails producing standardized products at low per-unit costs for price-sensitive consumers. Companies that strive to be the low-cost producers attempt to secure a mighty position in their marketplace. The low-cost producer can call the tune for the rest of the industry because of its cost advantages. Such a company can price its products low to gain market share or higher to secure a robust margin. In either case, a company successful at this strategy can become the dominant force in the industry and force other players to adjust to its decisions.

In order to be the low-cost producer, however, the organization must be relentless at pursuing efficiency and eliminating waste. Wal-Mart is the role model for the cost leadership strategy. In every aspect of operations—overhead expenditures, deals with suppliers, and store location and construction, Wal-Mart is single-minded about costs. As a result, Wal-Mart can boast in its ad campaigns, "Always the Low Price" or "Watch for Falling Prices." Wal-Mart is targeting price-sensitive buyers of everyday goods and it has been successful at securing customers who are loyal, principally because they know that the Wal-Mart price cannot be bettered.

Hallmarks of the management of the low-cost producer strategy are:

- Low overhead and limited executive perks
- Fanaticism regarding the elimination of waste
- Streamlined organizational structures with larger spans of control for managers
- Incentives based on cost controls, usually broadly implemented throughout the workforce
- `Tough negotiation of contracts with all suppliers

Low-cost producers are not casual about these management principles; they work at them every day and for the long haul. Of the three generic strategies, pursuing the low-cost position is the most difficult, because it requires true discipline, only one company can succeed, and the strategy is vulnerable to technological shifts.

Differentiator Strategy

If a company is not the low-cost producer, by definition, it must have an explanation for potential buyers as to why they should spend more than the lowest price. Whatever product or feature or benefit the company chooses to emphasize is its differentiation. The differentiation may be made on any component of the product, experience, or element of the buying process.

Key Term
Value proposition The rationale that companies adopt and utilize to guide their actions and their customers, in support of their strategy. It's a combination of all the benefits for customers that a company proposes to deliver at a specified price. The value proposition involves all the elements that constitute value as perceived by customers.

As we have seen, Starbucks and Target create an environment for customers that is their differentiation. Saturn differentiates itself on some of the features of its cars (like

> ### "The World's Finest Walking Shoes"
> Mephisto is an expensive brand of shoes. Mephisto's value proposition to customers is that there's no more comfortable shoe on the market and that the handmade comfort and durability of the product is well worth the price. Mephisto differentiates on its product design and use: the company states that its goal is "to create and manufacture the world's finest walking shoes." Style is almost secondary with Mephisto's strategy. Every shoe must first pass the test for ultimate walking comfort and fit.

crash-resistant door panels) and also on the no-haggle pricing aspect of the buying process to deliver value to customers.

The differentiation strategy is a must if we cannot compete effectively on price across the broad market. As we've noted, the cost leader must manage for expense control throughout the organization. Similarly, the differentiator must work its differentiation throughout all of its operations.

Niche Player Strategy

Niche players are companies that employ differentiation in their strategic design, but do so for a very targeted segment of the market. Niche players learn the detailed likes and dislikes of their customer base, focus differentiation to those characteristics, and do not attempt to reach outside the segment of choice.

Here's an example. Orvis of Vermont sells clothing, luggage, and footwear, among other things, but targets fly-fishing aficionados. Both its mail order business and its retail stores appeal to those who hunt and fish, own dogs, and long for a country gentry lifestyle. Orvis is quite content to be the vendor of choice for only that smallish segment.

Choosing and Committing

Generic strategies are a good way to begin to think about the direction and choices for our company to make in order to achieve its objectives. In developing the three generic strategies, Porter makes a strong point, based on evidence, that companies must choose one and only one of these three approaches. He advises companies to choose one strategy

Don't Be "Stuck in the Middle"

Porter notes that companies that mix a little cost leadership with differentiation or that may favor a market segment but not be dedicated to it are "stuck in the middle," in his terms. That's a prescription for failure. Kmart is a good example of being "stuck in the middle."

and then commit to it exclusively.

The key is to put together a comprehensive set of decisions that disperse the strategy throughout the business. By integrating the strategy everywhere in the organization, we reduce our chances of getting "stuck in the middle" and improve our chances of executing the strategy successfully.

Figure 6-1 shows the components of strategic options that reflect the need to drive the strategy to all parts of the business. It shows that complete strategy formulation requires two major components: positioning and execution and how effective strategy requires the alignment of the two components.

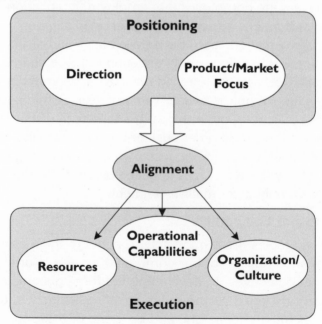

Figure 6-1. Components of strategic options

Positioning

By "positioning" we mean a concise and clear articulation of the company's strategic approach to achieving its goals. Positioning consists of two components: direction and product/market focus.

> **Positioning** Articulating clearly and concisely the company's strategic approach to achieving its goals. Positioning consists of two components: direction and product/market focus.

Strategic Direction

Strategic direction can be as simple as choosing one of the generic strategies. Alternatively, we may choose our business model as a direction, highlighting a key factor in the value chain.

For example, Dell Computer's direction is to go direct to customers. For Dell the key strategic direction is the distribution channel choice. Nordstrom's direction for achieving its goals is through intense customer service, more of a differentiation strategy.

Direction consists of components also. These components fit together to form the strategic direction that the company will pursue. The components of direction are:

- vision
- core values
- value proposition
- strategic plan
- consistent decision making

Vision and *values* clearly preside over the entire operation of the business; therefore, they take a prominent role in the development of the strategic direction for the future. It makes no sense to articulate vision and values, and then set them aside when we start formulating a strategy.

Our *value proposition* is the business link to the customer. Remember that in order for a business to be successful, it must convince customers to spend their cash for the products and

Kmart's Mixed Messages

Kmart was in the fight of its life with Wal-Mart. While Kmart couldn't beat Wal-Mart prices because, among other things, its supplier management was not as tough, still Kmart had to keep prices down. Yet, executive compensation at Kmart was inconsistent with cost management and well above the levels at Wal-Mart. As these choices became known, as they do in publicly traded companies, field employees became lukewarm to other cost reduction programs, which made those programs less effective.

services it offers. Without recognition of how and where we can create value to customers, which leads to transactions, we have no business. This is why customer analysis is such a critical part of formulating strategic direction.

Once a direction is chosen, we must lay out the plans for sequencing decisions and activities; this is the *strategic plan*. And finally, direction cannot be effective unless *decisions* are made (by top management and reinforced throughout the organization) that are *consistent* with the direction selected. If managers waffle on the direction by making choices that are inconsistent with the strategy, it weakens the company's effectiveness. Sadly, it doesn't take many inconsistent decisions for a strategy to collapse and die from the cynicism of stakeholders.

Product and Market Focus

The second piece of positioning lies in the choice of products and markets. The product aspect includes not only the design and features of the products or services that the company offers, but also the entire marketing mix. That means we formulate some notion about the pricing, promotion, and place (including geography and distribution channel) that makes the most sense. Market considerations mean that we decide on our scope, our customer segment—broad or focused.

Let's take an example that shows positioning in the choice of both products and markets. For Dell Computer, product initially meant personal desktop computers. Over time, it added laptops, digital cameras, printers, and other accessories to the mix. These items were added as a secondary strategy, to gain a bigger piece of the customer's technology spending rather than letting good and satisfied customers go to other vendors for these items. In the area of market choice, Dell initially targeted individual customers, but as success ensued, it added small and then big business customers to the segments of choice. As this business grew, Dell added servers and other products and services to accommodate the business segment.

These positioning choices are made based upon the analysis that preceded the strategic decision process—customer analysis, internal business analysis, SWOT, and external environmental study. Armed with the information that the research provides, we can choose and test various positioning combinations and evaluate which set of choices stands the best chance of succeeding.

Execution

It would be foolhardy, however, to make strategic positioning choices that could not be supported or executed by our skills, resources, and organization. That's why it's critical to align the positioning decisions with our capabilities and the realities of our situation. The components of our business that need to be aligned with the positioning fall into three categories:

- resources
- operational capabilities
- organization

In thinking about our company, we typically find that there is overlap among these categories, but the important thing to keep in mind is that we must consider the main components in formulating our strategy, regardless of which box they happen to fall into for housekeeping purposes.

Resources

Resources are our assets of people, property, and relationships. At the very least, the necessary resources to achieve the strate-

Put Time on Your Side

Smart Managing   Alignment among the components of strategy formulation requires a consideration of the timing of events and decisions. A public stock offering or the building of an R&D department is not deliverable instantaneously. In mapping out the path to implementing a strategy, make sure to fully consider the timing of the various important pieces. Often managers fail to plan properly, and conservatively, for the ramp-up of these capabilities and the execution of the strategy is spotty at best. As a consequence, results are not achieved. Create a realistic timeline of the important aligning factors in the rollout of the strategy and you'll have a better chance of making it work right.

gic intent have to be within reach of the organization, even if we do not have them at the present time.

For instance, a company that chooses to be a consolidator—that is, to acquire competitors to achieve size, scope, and scale in its industry—needs to have capital to buy these other firms. If the necessary capital is available currently, all well and good: it can proceed. However, even if the company does not have the funds currently, if it has access to the necessary capital, then it still can proceed with the strategy of consolidation. So, a company that lacks the required capital but has low debt or can raise funds through the public markets can embark on the acquisition approach knowing that it can accumulate the resources.

Similarly, a company that chooses to pursue an innovation strategy must have the R&D capabilities to make innovation possible. But that doesn't mean that it must have had a strong R&D function historically, if it can assemble one. An important and detailed examination of the firm's execution capability is recognizing the critical resources required by the positioning.

Here are seven categories of resources to consider when investigating strategic change:

- tangible assets
- access to financial capital
- access to human resources
- management talent
- intellectual capital

- brand and reputation
- technology

Operational Capabilities

Operating capabilities refer to the business processes in place in our organization that deliver the value proposition to the customer. We must be realistic in our assessment of these processes in order to determine whether a particular path will be possible.

Making the decision, for example, to be the low-cost producer requires extraordinary efficiencies in every aspect of the business. Some of our circumstances may not be changed easily and would thwart the company's ability to be successful in driving costs out of the business. If we cannot align our processes with the low-cost direction, then we must choose a different direction, probably differentiation.

Operational capabilities need to be examined across the entire value chain, from basic inputs to customer post-purchase services. By aligning the key drivers of success in our strategy with the business processes employed, we can determine whether or not a particular positioning will work.

Specific operating characteristics to consider in formulating strategy include the following:

- innovation capability
- design
- manufacturing skills

Capabilities Critical

Systems are often crucial to a company's strategies. Consider a local restaurant chain that wants to grow by expanding geographically. Without a scalable management and financial system, such a move would be very difficult, if not impossible. As the owners lose immediate and local control, communication links and business reports are required to provide good management to the remote locations. These systems are a necessary, but not sufficient, requirement for multiple location operations to succeed. Without them, management's ability to see problems, incent management, and monitor operations is severely restricted.

- entrepreneurship
- risk management
- sales strength
- ability to deliver for customers

Organization

Organization and culture issues cannot be ignored in our examination of strategic choices. One of the important considerations is
organizational design and structure. Firms that attempt to use
market-driven strategies, relying on factors like customer satisfaction or first-to-market advantages, would be likely to organize
around business units, rather than functional areas. With a business unit structure, full P&L (and value chain) responsibility can
be assigned to a single manager who can direct resources and
activities to achieve the best marketplace results. If responsibility
is diffused among several units (such as purchasing, manufacturing, and sales, for example), the structure might limit the ability
of the firm to fully deliver on the strategic promise.

Structure is not the only organizational concern. Culture
plays an important part in the execution capabilities of a business. Culture consists of a number of dimensions that define the
attitude and environment of the workplace. Pace of activity, risk
taking, and results orientation are three important considerations among many in defining a firm's culture. If the traditional

---

Form Follows Function

This old adage is borrowed from architecture, but it
applies to organizational design as well. The positioning
will determine what functionality we need; then we need to align the
structure with that intent.

A strategy that seeks fast and strong top-line growth may require
use of an external sales system (manufacturers' reps or independent
distributors, for example), for a closer and faster link between market
introduction and sales. Furthermore, using outside sales requires pay-
ments to the sales force only when a sale takes place, which makes
the sales area purely a variable cost and frees up resources to expand
production as required to deliver the unit growth.

> ### Can You Teach an Old Dog New Tricks?
> Because of the difficulty associated with bringing change to a corporate culture quickly, one way to accomplish the alignment between positioning and culture is to form a new entity. Firms can sometimes bypass the challenges of trying to transform the old organization by establishing a new entity, probably a subsidiary, and creating the culture of choice in the new structure. The new unit may take a new name and brand, new operating processes, and new employees. Delta Airlines has created Song, its new, low-priced service, for exactly this reason.

pace of activity is deliberate, it would be difficult to adopt a strategy direction like first-to-market that required a much faster execution of activities.

You should evaluate these six factors of the organization in the strategic design:

- structure
- leadership strength
- teamwork
- ability to motivate
- pace of activity
- center of organizational power

Aligning Resources, Operational Capabilities, and Organization

The notion of aligning positioning with execution simply means that we will pick a strategy only if we can deliver it to the marketplace through the resources, capabilities, and design of our organization. In order to achieve this strategic success, we must examine the resources, operational capabilities, and

> ### Positioning Is Not Enough
> Too often strategy is mistaken for marketing. A firm's advertising campaign is seen as its strategy. Companies need marketing strategies within their business strategies, but even that is not enough. The lesson from successful businesses is that the important activity in formulating a business strategy is aligning our direction and goals with the organization's ability to execute.

organization and, if necessary, redesign them to properly align with the strategic design. This means that in every nook and cranny the elements of the organization are all operating in line with the strategy.

Classes of Strategies

Porter's three generic strategies are a good starting place for creating a comprehensive business strategy, but strategy development requires more. To develop a successful plan, managers must answer a simple question: How? For example, if we choose to pursue a cost leadership approach to our markets, we need to ask further, How do we do that? The answer may lie in product design or it may lie in scale economies or in may lie in production efficiencies. Similarly if we choose to apply a differentiation strategy, we again need to ask, How? Will we differentiate on quality, valued-added services, or our product line offerings?

The strategic choices are nearly endless. Every company's unique combination of positioning and execution can lead to another unique strategy. Yet, there are some common strategic approaches that we can identify that will help to define the best formulation for our particular company. These are the common classes of strategy:

- integration
- market penetration
- market development
- product development
- diversification
- joint venturing
- divestiture

These categories of strategy are useful in exploring our choices. Like the generic strategies, these groupings help managers develop the correct approach for their specific goals and circumstances.

Integration Strategies

Integration strategies are about control. As a company grows, opportunities arise to gain control of some aspects of the value chain that historically were outside the control of the company. There are three forms of integration: forward, backward, and horizontal. *Forward* integration actions look toward the customer end of the value chain for prospects. Typically, forward integration includes acquiring distribution or customer service activities. *Backward* integration seeks to find benefits toward the supplier end of the value chain. For example, a distributor might look backward to gain control of a key manufacturer. Of course, forward and backward perspectives depend upon what activities the company is currently engaged in actively. *Horizontal* integration means gaining control of competitors. Horizontal integration is commonly referred to as consolidation or a rollup strategy.

Before we ask, How do we integrate?, it's critical to explore why we might use an integration strategy.

Forward integration is typically used to protect or increase sales. Have you noticed how many catalog retailers are now opening retail stores? Harry and David, Lands' End, and Crate and Barrel all are examples of companies that have integrated forward in the value chain. The brick-and-mortar presence in strong markets not only creates growth opportunities, but also keeps the brand visible so catalog sales maintain their momentum.

Almost all of the major U.S. car companies have

Holding Back in Retail Stores

TRICKS OF THE TRADE

Not all goods in catalog vendors' lines are available in the physical store. Pottery Barn, Eddie Bauer, and many others hold back goods as "catalog only." Why? Because these companies want to keep the catalog operation vibrant. By holding back goods, they guide customers to look at and order from the catalog. By doing so, the companies keep their investments in the catalog operations continuing to generate sales and they keep both channels alive.

at one time or another invested in the rental car business: Ford in Hertz, GM in National, and Chrysler in Thrifty. This is a forward integration strategy to protect their access to sales of large fleets to the rental business. Through their investment, the auto companies ensured a level of orders for rental cars from their aligned rental companies.

Backward integration looks to gain more control of suppliers. The rationale for backward integration typically involves ensuring supply, exclusivity, and pricing conditions, as well as, in some cases, greater ability to align and forecast production. General Electric has encouraged selective use of backward integration with its customers. Home Depot has established strong integration with GE on appliances. If you buy a GE appliance at Home Depot, the salesperson looks right into the GE inventory and production system. The appliance then is shipped directly to an independent delivery company that takes care of getting the appliance delivered and installed. For Home Depot, this backward integration eliminates significant warehousing. For GE, this forward integration strategy, means solid pricing and production forecasting improvements.

Forward and backward integration opportunities are called *supply chain management.* Supply chain management looks at the relationships along the continuum of suppliers-manufacturer-distributors to find creative ways to increase revenue and reduce costs. Of course, one of the big new areas of supply chain management is the introduction of e-commerce and the use of the Internet along the supply chain.

Horizontal integration is a little bit different from forward and backward approaches. In horizontal integration, the company is gaining control of competitors. The trends in corporate acquisitions are increasing, for various reasons. Sometimes consolidation occurs to increase size and scope, to gain economies of scale or operational efficiency. Often competitors are acquired to directly achieve revenue growth. In other cases, competitors are acquired to obtain execution capabilities, like systems, technology, intellectual capital, or access to new distribution. Philip

Morris (now Altria Group) is reported to have purchased Kraft Foods simply to acquire more management competencies in the food business, a skill set that the company identified as a weakness.

Market Penetration Strategies

When growth is the objective, we might ask, How can we build market share in the products and markets that we currently serve? Looking for share means we're exploring a market penetration strategy, that is, selling more of what we sell in the markets we're selling in!

The key to market penetration is customer knowledge. If we've done a good job at customer analysis, we will know where the opportunities for increased penetration of the market lie and then, as Nike says, we must *just do it!*

Market Development Strategies

When a business has done all that it reasonably can in a particular market, but growth in that market is not sufficient to achieve the company's objectives, it's time to look to new markets. When we explore bringing our business to new markets, that's market development. Restaurant chains—pick one: Olive Garden, P.F. Chang's, Chili's, or Applebee's—all have employed market development strategies. Once a restaurant has established a successful business model (menu, execution, style, environment, décor, and so forth), the path to growth lies in expansion into new markets. Geographic expansion then requires selecting sites, developing systems and suppliers, and promoting aggressively. Hotels and almost all retail establishments choose market development strategies because the catchment area for retail is very localized.

Globalization is now a common strategic thrust of many companies. Globalization can be categorized as international market development. However, firms considering expansion to new countries must be mindful of cultural differences and customer/market idiosyncrasies. In Mexico, for example, it's difficult to make a strong market presence without sponsorship by or

---

Franchising Market Development

Smart Managing   One technique for entering new markets is to find partners that will help finance and operate the new business location. Franchising does exactly that. If we have a stable, consistent business model and a strong or rising brand, franchising can be a fast and effective method for opening new markets. U.S. franchise sales amount to about $1 trillion. Hotels, restaurants, distribution companies, and retail shops dominate the franchise business, but there are other possibilities. The flip side of the franchising movement is that companies do not own all of the growth and profit generated by the franchisees. Just as operations and financing are shared, so is profit.

---

affiliation with one of the major existing Mexican companies. Disney found that moving Disney-land to the suburbs of Paris was not a sure success without real efforts to accommodate French and European culture.

Product Development Strategies

Product development is necessary as a natural result of the product life cycle. The life cycle concept suggests that products go through several phases. When products are introduced to meet unmet needs, adoption is slow at first. But if the product is successful, the sales of the product will increase and the business will grow. Then, over time, competitors or substitutes come along to chip away at the sales. Ultimately the market tires of the product and seeks alternatives.

The length of the phases of the cycle varies according to the product, the market, and other factors. Fads are characterized by fast adoption, growth, and fast deterioration. Other products have an extremely long life cycle and remain unchanged for decades. For example, Wheaties, Ivory Soap, and Pennzoil all are products that have been marketed for years, essentially unchanged. But that's not to say that these products still hold the same share of the market that they once did. Synthetic oil, like Mobil 1, has put pressure on Pennzoil to introduce synthetic oil. In fact, each of these companies has led or responded to product developments to keep their corporate place in the market secure.

Diversification Strategies

Individual investors know what diversification means, particularly after the technology stock collapse of 2000. For our portfolio of investments, it makes sense to place our money into diverse assets so that if one or two areas fall, other investments will make up the difference. Companies, too, can diversify, so that if one business falters, unrelated businesses can continue and perhaps compensate. Companies that amalgamate companies in diverse products and markets are called conglomerates.

Today this notion of diversification, the conglomerate, is out of fashion, principally because results of these companies have been poor. Most observers found that operating multiple businesses in vastly different product/market sectors was too difficult. The dissimilar business models, skill sets, and resource requirements tended to create a complex organization that was difficult to administer.

Yet, diversification still can be a useful strategy. Two companies that have excelled using what appears to be a diversification strategy are General Electric and Fortune Brands. General Electric operates in appliances, light bulbs, complex medical equipment, power plants, financial services, and aircraft engines. Fortune Brands includes companies like Titleist Golf, Jim Beam, Moen, Wilson-Jones, and Masterlock, among others. Why are these models successful? The answer lies in the fact that both companies have a unifying concept across the entire organization.

For GE, the unifying concept is the operating discipline of the organization. While the businesses are diverse, GE operates each using similar principles of six sigma, flattened organizational structures, and a management focus on results and specific values.

Fortune Brands has a different unifying concept, brand management. Each of its companies has a strong brand and all companies are managed around a singular brand management approach, even though the products are in very different markets.

The failure of diversification as a strategy has led to a reexamination of the approach on two fronts. One is the notion that companies don't need to diversify if investors do. Investors seek returns and can buy multiple stocks to achieve the necessary risk management of their portfolios; therefore, companies don't need to diversify. The second factor is the notion of core competencies. We will explore core business identification and focus in Chapter 8, but research shows that companies that focus on single businesses areas do better than diversified businesses. The conclusion is that companies should exploit their strengths and stick to one core business.

Joint Venturing Strategies

A joint venture (JV) is a new organization built through the combined resources of two or more existing entities. Figure 6-2 depicts the essence of a JV.

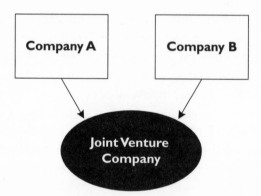

Figure 6-2. The essence of a joint venture

A typical JV story goes something like this. An innovative business idea is born, but the company lacks some of the resources, technology, operating capabilities, or structures to make it work. The company then seeks to partner with another firm, which has the missing ingredients. The two companies form a joint venture company, which is managed independently, but supervised by a board of directors contributed by each of

---

The First Mission in Joint Venturing
TRICKS OF THE TRADE

Question: What is the first consideration in a joint venture?
Answer: How do we get out of the deal? Because JVs are difficult to design, operate, and sustain, it's vital that the founders agree on an exit structure. Each party may be given the right to buy the other out at a formula price. Or, alternatively, the JV can be dissolved with some notice. In any event, creating a viable and reasonable exit from a JV is an important early consideration, particularly if the plans for success do not materialize.

---

the founding entities. Nokia, 3i Group, Accenture, and Sampo partnered in 2001 to form Meridea Financial Software, a JV that will develop mobile and on-line financial software. Meridea will use the expertise of its founders to create products that make financial services applications more accessible globally through a variety of technology mechanisms, including the Internet, mobile phones, and digital TV.

If we partner with other companies for products or services without forming a new entity, then we call that arrangement a *strategic alliance.* Toyota's provision of drive trains for certain GM vehicles, for example, is a strategic alliance.

Divestiture Strategies

Sometimes there's no way out but out. That's when a divestiture strategy makes sense. Divestiture typically refers to the sale of a product line or business unit. Retrenchment is the term used when a company simply discontinues an operation or business activity. IBM recently discontinued selling its desktop PCs through retail outlets like CompUSA and Circuit City, opting instead to sell only directly through its own online distribution system. Microsoft divested itself of Expedia, its travel operation, after experiencing poor results. In many cases, divestiture is another recognition that companies must focus on core operations. Alternatively, divestitures can be made to convert capital from weak businesses and to invest the proceeds in better opportunities.

On to Strategic Thinking

The seven strategic choices just outlined are not a comprehensive list, but provide a starting point for thinking about the strategic choices for our own company. In the next three chapters, I detail three specific techniques for spawning the strategic thinking necessary to formulate a successful strategy within our company:

- optimizing assets
- core business analysis
- 10 tested business strategies

Manager's Checklist for Chapter 6

❏ Generic strategies of cost leadership, differentiation, and niche player provide a good foundation for the strategic choices each business faces.

❏ We must choose one of the generic strategies and not fall into being "stuck in the middle."

❏ Our comprehensive strategy is made up of positioning and execution.

❏ It's critical to align our positioning approach with our execution capabilities throughout the organization.

❏ To enhance our strategic choices, we ask the question: How?

❏ We develop strategy by looking at the opportunities to reach our goals through various approaches, like integration, penetration, development, diversification, and divestiture.

Strategic Thinking: Optimizing Assets

United Airlines flight 1203 leaves Chicago's O'Hare Airport at 7:45 p.m. and arrives at Sky Harbor Airport in Phoenix at 9:20 p.m. Theoretically, anyway, no matter how many people show up for this flight, off the plane goes for its nightly trip. Obviously, this flight, and every other scheduled flight, involves predominately fixed costs. It may be a little more expensive to fly the plane full than half-full, but not much more in relative terms.

Recognizing these relationships, years ago the airlines came up with a plan to help fill every plane. It was a simple but radical idea—give away the empty seat free of charge! The one catch was that, in order to get the free seat, customers would have to give up shopping around for air travel and become loyal to one airline. Thus frequent flyer programs were born.

If the airlines wanted to create customer loyalty, the success of the frequent flyer programs is unqualified. Customers who historically valued the schedule, number of transfers, price, recommendation of a travel agent, and type of equipment, now valued one factor more than any other: the airline (and its miles). At a time when the volume of travel was increasing greatly, most airlines saw great dividends from instituting these programs.

The concept behind the frequent flyer programs is simply to maximize the use of the asset. If the plane isn't full, give away the seats as a reward for filling the seats on some other flights. Airlines also aggressively sold space in the fuselage of the planes to the Postal Service and small cargo carriers of all types. Since the flight was going from Chicago to Phoenix any-way, fill it up as much as possible.

So the airlines traded a few free seats for a system that rewards customer loyalty. While at first this appears to be a short-term tactic for building occupancy on the flights, this approach was instrumental in changing the business model that the major airlines adopted. Thus, by looking at increasing the use of their assets (the airplanes), the airlines developed a new strategy.

Asset Optimization

Asset optimization began with the development of the old DuPont formula of the 1920s for analyzing profits. Return on assets measures the level of profitability of a business relative to the level of investment in assets:

$$ROA = \frac{Profit}{Total\,Assets}$$

An ROA of 15% means that for every $1 worth of assets the firm's processes yielded 15 cents of profit. The better assets were utilized, the more profit was yielded per dollar of asset investment. But the DuPont notion broke down this ROA con-cept into component pieces:

$$ROA = \frac{Profit}{Sales} \times \frac{Sales}{Total\,Assets}$$

By looking at this decomposition of the ROA, we see that it depends upon profit per sale, or the profit margin, times the asset turnover ratio. Asset turnover reflects the conversion of our business assets into transactions, in money terms. The more transactions, or sales, per unit asset, the better our assets are being utilized.

When we think about these concepts in today's environment, two thoughts come to mind.

First, with technology, globalization of markets, and levels of competition, profit margins in most industries are getting squeezed very tightly. For most companies, the cost of making a sale in the crowded arena is high and prices are very difficult to raise. If, then, we want to improve our ROA, assuming margins are going down, asset turns must increase. We must come up with ideas to generate more sales per unit of assets.

The second observation is that the only number in this formulation that's understated is the asset figure. Because these are accounting-based measures, asset levels are depreciated and do not include much value for the intangible assets. Intangible assets include people, customer and supplier relationships, intellectual capital, and others. Accounting assets also do not fully reflect property that is not owned, but controlled by the firm. So, since the asset level in the calculation is understated, so are our returns; therefore, we need to get even more from each and every asset to achieve adequate returns.

The bottom line is that asset management and optimization have been around a long time as tools for measuring performance. We want to apply these concepts to finding new business ideas and strategies. Clearly, the options are based on getting more from the same level of assets or finding ways to reduce assets and still garner the same, or better, returns.

The asset optimization approach to developing strategy is based on the idea that if we look at each and every significant asset and think about how to make the best use of that asset, we may find new strategies for our business. We begin with this method for strategic thinking because it is based on what we already have, our existing set of assets. Before we think about new things, why not try and find ways to fully utilize the assets that we currently own or control?

Finding Cash Flow in Assets

In the late 1980s, the University of Wisconsin-Madison's athletic department faced a $2 million deficit. Football revenues were significantly off due to dismal performance in the Big Ten. Basketball and hockey were not making up the difference, so new ideas were needed.

Even with Barry Alvarez as the new football coach, Pat Richter, the new athletic director, knew that it would be at least a couple of years before the football program turned around and the stadium filled again.

Camp Randall Stadium in Madison seats 80,000 and sits right in the middle of campus. It is a huge asset of the university, yet it was only used six or seven times a year for home football games. Richter decided to optimize the stadium asset. He booked concerts (Pink Floyd and the Rolling Stones) and events like Drum Corps International into the stadium. The asset generated more income and helped to fill the budget deficit. Over time, concert and event revenue from all the facilities became an important component of the athletic department business model. Of course, more importantly, the football team won three Rose Bowls in 10 years and the stadium filled up for all home football games.

Asset Categories

In the simple model of business described earlier, there are three categories of assets: people, property, and relationships. We'll look at each group to find ideas that use the assets better and lead to achieving our goals. In each case, we need to identify the key assets, evaluate their current use, and ask how that use might be increased. In our review, we'll look to enhance some assets, reduce or eliminate some assets, or convert some assets from one type to another.

People

The first step is to identify the key groups of people affiliated with the organization. The categories might reflect a type of employee or a departmental staff. Types of employees might be managers, executives, or salespeople. A simple grouping is line versus staff. Departments include the usual list along the value chain—purchasing, R&D, IT, production, logistics, service, and sales. In some cases, where functions are outsourced, the people are not employees, for example, using manufacturers' representatives for the sales function.

The objective of this exercise is not to review the performance of any individual, but rather to examine whether these resources can be used more effectively and to generate better results. If we can determine initiatives to help the organization achieve its goals, then that's a strategy worth considering and we should put it on the list of possible initiatives. Some potential people initiatives are:

- pay-for-performance incentives
- outsourcing
- workout
- building a business around an expertise

Pay-for-Performance Incentives. If we determine that a group of people can be driven to higher performance by paying them more based on performance, then it's a strategy that we should consider. In general, pay-for-performance programs share with a group of employees some of the benefits of reaching particular goals, so payment is made only if the value is created through the operations of the company. Pay-for-performance systems can be found in many forms, including:

- broad-based profit-sharing plans
- individual or team bonus programs
- stock option grants
- special incentive programs

Profit-sharing plans, cash or deferred, provide money for employees or their retirement funds, based on the achievement of a specific profit target. In most cases, profit sharing is applied across the whole company, but targets and payouts can be varied by unit or division.

Individual bonus plans are used almost universally with executives and more senior managers. In these cases, specific targets can be set for the manager's area of responsibility. By

The Down Side of Profit Sharing

Profit-sharing plans can be very helpful to augment pay for employees. However, there are some problems that may arise.

Plans that never or seldom pay out are not motivational. Employees tend to think that such plans are designed to not pay out or they don't link their own hard work to a benefit. A similar problem arises whenever the payout is based on consolidated results in multi-divisional companies. Successful units and unsuccessful ones could be rewarded to the same extent, even though individual unit performance varies, because the combined results were good. Finally, some profit-sharing plans that pay out well regularly become taken for granted, and an entitlement attitude develops.

raising the expectations, performance can be improved. On the other side, however, individual goals tend to make people think only about their operations and some opportunities for synergies may be difficult to deliver.

Stock option grants are used widely in publicly traded firms, particularly in the technology sector. Option grants typically vest over four to five years and permit the holder to purchase stock at a fixed price so that in the future when the grant is exercised any price increase in the stock inures to the holder.

For example, David was granted 10,000 options to purchase stock in his company at $15 per share. The options vest in four years. David is permitted to exercise the options at any time, up to 12 years after the grant. After 10 years, David wants to send a child to college and needs some cash. The current stock price is $65 a share. In essence, David gets $50 per share or $500,000.

Vesting For participants in employee stock option plans, earning the right to exercise their rights.

In the case of options that vest in four years, for example, the grant is made today, but the recipient does not own the options until four years have passed and, typically, is still working for the company. Vesting over time is used to ensure that employees will remain with the company and not "take the money and run."

Options on Options

How do you handle employee stock options? In the wake of accounting scandals in which corporations used stock options to avoid paying taxes while overstating their earnings, the Financial Accounting Standards Board has been pushing to require companies to expense stock options.

Proponents of the idea argue that options are a form of compensation and should be recorded as expenses. However, many companies oppose the idea for two reasons. First, options provide future benefits based upon successful innovations in very complex and high-capital-investment businesses. Options provide both rewards for good intellectual capital ideas and retention benefits, since most option grants vest over a long period of time. The second reason is that there's not a very good way to value the cost of options, in real terms.

It may be a while before the dust settles in this conflict. This is an area where strategies may develop to keep up with regulations.

Options align employees' interests with the stockholders' interests. Stockholders make money on their investments in a company if the company creates value. Option grants are intended to remind employees that they need to create value for the shareholders.

Special incentive programs are ways to motivate employees to ensure that a particular job gets done. In many firms, very large projects, like installing a new ERP system, involve multi-functional task forces from all over the organization. It's not uncommon for the teams to have special incentives for an on-time delivery of the system.

Outsourcing. Outsourcing functions or activities has been a very common trend in business. The reason? Specialists, focused on a particular service, develop expertise and efficiency regarding the area that people within companies cannot match with their levels of performance and cost. As a result, departments that traditionally have been part of the companies' services are dismantled and the activities that they handled are outsourced to specialty firms.

TRICKS
OF THE
TRADE
Outsource All of Your Employees

Professional employer organizations (PEOs), also called employee-leasing companies, essentially co-employ a company's employees. The PEO takes responsibility for all HR functions like payroll and benefits administration, risk management, staffing, and compliance. Most PEOs are targeted at smaller businesses that don't have and don't want employees and the hassles associated with these functions.

Call centers are a great example. It's expensive to invest in a call center and difficult and expensive to operate and manage it. Getting and keeping call center employees is challenging. Training, attendance issues, and call center technology are all even more reasons why some companies have found that it's easier to manage a single call center vendor to specific targets than to manage 100 call center employees.

Almost any functional area can be outsourced. When management believes that an area is too much trouble for the benefits delivered to the business value proposition, the area is a candidate for outsourcing. Outsourcing, so the argument goes, relieves managers from ancillary or noncritical functions, so they can focus on the more important activities that create value.

Workout. Workout is the General Electric term for getting the organization out of the employees' way so they can be more

The Virtual Insurance Company

An insurance company can be formed today without any employees; the entire business can be outsourced. Insurance companies have five major tasks: sales, policy administration, asset management, claims, and customer service. Sales can be done by independent agents, policy administration can be handled by a reinsurance company, asset managers are a dime a dozen, several independent claims adjuster companies would compete for the business, and customer service can be covered through a call center and by agents. No employees!

productive. One of the reasons that people in our organization may not be as optimized as we would like is that the bureaucracy and their bosses will not allow them to operate at their best. Whether it's paperwork or policy or the old "'mother, may I?' syndrome" of companies that do not empower their employees, most organizations have obstacles that they could reduce or eliminate.

Robert Slater, in his book, *The GE Way Fieldbook*, explains the history and techniques of Workout. Suffice it to say that the approach has worked wonders at GE: Jack Welch says it's one of the best things that he did at GE. But it requires a systematic and comprehensive effort. In Workout, the problem is not the people, but the organization.

Building a Business Around an Expertise. In looking at our people assets, we may discover real expertise that has value beyond the walls of the existing company. For example, Kimberly-Clark ran its in-house airline (K-C Aviation) so well that the company converted it into a commercial airline, called Midwest Express. The expertise may be in engineering or in design, in running a call center or operating power plants. In a sense, this is the reverse of outsourcing. A true expertise may be the seeds of a new business. Finding and then testing such

Defense Department Golf Clubs?

Bob Bettinardi ran a company that milled parts for, among others, the Department of Defense, using a state-of-the-art milling process called CNC (computer numerically controlled). CNC permitted extremely accurate milling of metals to exacting specifications. Bob, a golfer, one day looked at the latest and greatest putter and noticed that the milling of the face was not done using CNC technology. Bob had the machinery, his staff had the expertise, and so Bettinardi Golf was begun. Its principal product is putters. Recently two events proved the value of his move: he entered into a long-term agreement to make equipment for the Ben Hogan Company and his putter was used to win the 2003 U.S. Open. He turned expertise into a business.

an enterprise is hard work, but the result may provide great opportunities in new markets, with outstanding growth and profit potential.

Property

Property is the second category of assets that we can try to optimize to find new strategies. Again, we begin by identify the key property assets of the organization. Property categories include the following:

- land and buildings
- equipment and inventory
- technology
- financial assets
- products
- brands

There are two questions to consider in reviewing the property assets for optimization. First, can we increase use of the asset or better configure it so that it generates more return? (Putting concerts in the football stadium is an example.) The second question relates to the nature of the asset. Is there anything special or unique about it that makes it valuable in more than one circumstance? If the answer to either of these questions is yes, then maybe there's a new strategy waiting to be uncovered by exploring the possibilities.

Land and Buildings. Look around some old cities or towns. Often you will see the faded image of an advertisement painted on a prominent side of a building. Using space for advertising and generating additional revenue from that activity is almost as old an optimizing technique as business itself. Farmers rented parts of their land near highways for billboards. Web sites like Yahoo rent e-space to companies for banners and pop-up ads. Busses, subways, stadiums, professional athletes and racecar drivers, and long-haul trucks all use unused space on their property to sell to advertisers to make their physical assets more valuable.

Tiger Woods gets paid handsomely to have his golf bag, which gets lots of TV airtime, embroidered with the Buick name. Movie producers fight off competitors and sell product use in their films to the highest bidder. Did you see Julia Roberts drinking that Coke? Well, Coke outbid Pepsi for that right. Not all of these examples are of land and buildings, but they all reflect the value that advertisers see in the opportunity to promote their products in unique venues.

Land and buildings, of course, also can be optimized when unused space is leased out to other companies for their use. Albertsons grocery stores believed that the size of its typical store was large enough for all the groceries and other items it was selling and also for a Starbucks coffee outlet. Wal-Mart does the same with McDonald's. These stores recognize that these leases do two things: generate revenue and create more traffic for their stores.

Equipment and Inventory. Southwest Airlines is one of the few air carriers that consistently make money. There are lots of reasons why. Southwest has truly differentiated its business model for air travel. One of the key ingredients to that success is an equipment decision. Southwest buys and flies only one type of airplane, the Boeing 737. By standardizing its equipment, Southwest takes a great deal of cost out of the traditional air carrier's system. Pilots need to train on only one aircraft. Baggage handlers can work more effectively. Parts

Hospitals Go Southwest

Smart Managing

Many hospitals are seeing the value of the standardized equipment decision for Southwest Airlines. Hospitals are increasingly choosing only one manufacturer of artificial hips, knees, and other surgical implants. This standardization reduces training costs for nurses and doctors. It also makes surgical procedures more similar, reducing the problems of patient care and recovery. Doctors, used to making these decisions independently, typically resist these decisions to standardize, but the demand for health care cost controls and better outcomes encourages hospitals to fully examine the choice.

One Man's Ceiling Is Another Man's Floor

T.J. Maxx, Ross Stores, Stein Mart, and Marshall's have each created a business because of excess inventory. Department stores, big retailers, and soft goods manufacturers are slaves to fashion. As the seasons change, whatever is left over, after deep discounting, is passé. These firms need to sell the latest goods and are willing to sell the excess inventories to stores like Ross, at sharply cut prices, just to take the goods off the floor. These stores then remarket the goods as their own with nice markups over their cost, but at much lower prices than the primary retailers.

inventories are reduced substantially compared with other airline service shops. And planes can be repaired more quickly and reliably.

Inventory, like most assets, is a risk. A company that maintains big inventories is vulnerable to new products and improvements that make it difficult for it to get full pricing. For large items, inventory becomes a storage nightmare. Warehouses and trucking or other logistics expenses will eat up margins quickly. Just-in-time systems coordinate supply and demand to reduce or eliminate some of these costs and risks of inventory.

Technology. Most firms have invested heavily in all kinds of technology. In some cases, the technology is being fully utilized; in others, the assets are not generating as much income as possible. If we walk through the offices of many companies, you will see a personal computer on every desk. If we delve into the uses of those computers, we find that they are often used for Internet access, word processing, and spreadsheet applications only. Each machine is fully loaded with software and capabilities to do much more, but generally that capacity is wasted. Thin client hardware and software companies (like Citrix Systems) scale the power of desktop systems to the specific needs of the business and reduce costs significantly.

Financial Assets. Cash management is all about making the most of holding cash—investing in short-term liquid interest-bearing assets, collecting receivables quickly, and converting

eBay's Scalable Technology

eBay created quite a powerhouse Internet business. Translating an auction system to the Net, eBay has permitted thousands of individual consumers to attempt to sell goods in a global, digital classified ad. But eBay has done more.

Because its systems have capacity and appeal, hundreds if not thousands of retailers now also sell on the eBay site. So, for example, car dealerships now have a national market for their used cars. Vendors have noticed that "early adopters," those consumers who are willing to purchase new goods more readily, are attracted to eBay. As a result, if you're looking for the latest models of almost any product, you probably can find it on eBay. These early adopters are also often willing to pay premium prices for new or unique products, so the value of using eBay is enhanced.

noncash items into cash through factoring or other techniques. The idea of cash management is to make your company's cash work harder for you. We should treat all of our financial assets in the same way.

Financial strength and skill are valuable assets. Two of the more powerful financial assets are our debt capacity and rating and our stock price. Firms with good credit can move more quickly, to seize opportunities immediately and create value at a moment's notice. Banks can be very generous to companies with strong balance sheets.

On the other hand, a high stock price is a valuable commodity, particularly as a currency used in acquisitions. Suppose the managers of company X are willing to sell to us for $20 per share. We tender an offer to their board to purchase the entire company in which they will take our shares as payment. If our stock price were $20 per share, we would exchange on a one-for-one basis. But if our stock price rose to $40 per share before the closing, we would have to exchange only half as many shares to gain control of company X.

Products. How can we generate more from our products? Microsoft of the early '90s provides a good lesson. At the time, the best-selling software for personal computers was,

Private Equity Funds Use Financial Assets Well

Smart Managing

Private equity funds are pools of money put together by individuals, foundations, and corporations. These funds seek out ownership and control of early-stage businesses (usually strapped for money) or struggling companies with good ideas (usually strapped for money). The funds try to buy smart and manage hard, pushing both new-growth companies and turnaround to achieve outstanding results. If things go well, after a relatively short time, five years or less, the funds look to convert their stock investment to cash by selling the company. Then, restocked with even more cash and handsome returns, these financially powerful entities begin the process again.

Many corporations, seeking to copy the fine results of the equity funds, have created their own funds. Typically these funds are used to gain interests in new firms in related industries or supporting technologies of use to the sponsoring corporation. Remember what your mother told you: it takes money to make money!

by category:

- word processing: WordPerfect
- data base: dBase
- spreadsheet: Lotus 1-2-3
- presentation: Harvard Graphics

Today the unqualified leader in PC software applications is Microsoft Office Suite, a bundle of all four types of software and more. The names listed above are mostly gone from the radar screen.

How did this transformation take place? It may have been unintentional, like so many business successes, but Microsoft decided to put its software (Word, Access, Excel, PowerPoint) on the same software platform. Because sales were not great, management wanted to reduce developer expenses and increase speed to market. Using the same platform created a user benefit in ease of use. The stroke of genius, however, was that the same platform enabled the company to bundle the software ... and the rest is history,

Another very famous product story is the 3M Post-it® Note innovation. This hugely successful product was the result of a glue experiment that didn't actually work out as intended, because of a lack of adhesion. But a perceptive scientist saw the application on small paper notes—and lemons turned into lemonade for 3M.

These examples highlight the opportunity for companies to find new ideas in their current products and the ways in which they are constructed, marketed, and used. By exploring the possibilities in a creative environment, companies can find new ways to create value.

Brands. The great thing about a brand is that it is, by definition, unique. Brands also convey a message and a bundle of expectations about the products or services bearing that mark. Good brands yield competitive advantage. Our brand assets are very valuable and we need to protect them. But in many circumstances, the brand can be extended to a broader set of products and therefore create value.

In Chapter 2, Starbucks' mission was reported to become "the premier purveyor of the finest coffee in the world." Even before it reaches that goal, Starbucks is using its brand to sell coffee-related items. Two examples are Starbucks ice cream, in a few coffee-influenced flavors, and Starbucks Frappuccino, sold in markets and convenience stores. In both

---

Brand Extension Opportunities

Hewlett-Packard has a very strong position in computer printers. The HP brand on a printer is strong and carries a message of quality, reliability, ease of use, and durability. HP has leveraged its strength in all formats: ink-jet, color, and laser technologies. As digital photography has improved in quality and cost, HP has produced printers designed to deliver photographs. But HP did not stop there. HP had the know-how and capability to design and market digital cameras. While not a strong player in the camera market, compared with Canon and Nikon, HP has used its brand and market influence to fill out the line of products associated with digital photography from start to finish.

cases, the Starbucks brand gets seen and experienced in more and broader settings, thereby building its value.

By optimizing the use of its property, a company can build value. To find strategic initiatives in property assets, we look at the nature of the asset and all possible alternative uses to determine whether a new business idea and a new source of income are available from the asset.

Relationships

Commercial relationships are an important part of every company's business model. There are three relationships that we look at:

- customer relationships
- supplier relationships
- government relationships

Customer Relationships. The most important relationship that we own is with the customer. When we look for new strategic initiatives, the customer is, or should be, a very high-potential candidate. Why? First, customers know us and, if they like us, we can influence them. Second, we know them, or at least we should. We should know something of their likes and dislikes, demographics, and buying behaviors. Armed with this information, can we get more from this association than we currently are able to garner? How?

One method is to sell the customers. Companies commonly sell their customer lists to others as an additional source of revenue. Whether this use of customer information is well regarded by the customers is certainly in question. Another method is to sell the customer again, but under our umbrella. In your bank or credit card statements, you'll often see solicitations for services offered by the bank or sometimes others. Airlines have partnered with companies, both travel-related (rental cars, hotels, cell phone services) and not (credit cards, for example), so that mileage programs are connected to purchasing these other services. Airlines form these partnerships

> ## GE Medical Systems Reaches for Customers
> General Electric's Medical Systems division sells products like X-ray machines, scanners, MRIs, and monitoring equipment to hospitals and medical centers. GE is not content, however. It regularly uses acquisitions to increase its penetration of the market (more customers), its share of a particular hospital's capital equipment budget (bigger share of current customers' wallets), and to cross-sell new services (like consulting). GE's goal is to be the preferred supplier of capital goods and related services to the medical market. GE uses both its market power to influence sales and its business processes, like Six Sigma, to drive competitive advantage to its products and value to its customers.

to take advantage of their relationships with current customers.

One activity that is useful in multi-divisional companies is to share the customer lists and jointly determine which customers might also be well suited for the other divisions or business units. Veolia Environnement is a French utility services company that sells principally to governments. Services like operating water systems, public transportation, and waste management are contained in its product portfolio. One obvious strategy is to use its customer relationships in one division to increase sales in others.

Supplier Relationships. Suppliers—whether on the input, administrative, or sales sides of the business—can be powerful allies in creating new strategies for growth and profit. Most companies today are limiting their supply arrangements, creating stronger and deeper relationships with firms that they trust and that can deliver the products and services that meet their needs. Strong customer relationships are the best way to secure good supplier arrangements, so suppliers know that their partner has good volume and a strong business model.

Optimizing our supplier relationships means finding value for our company and our customers in those relationships. Increasing value to the company means creating a regular, predictable source of supply with consistent quality and advantaged

HMOs and Medical Groups: A Powerful Supplier Relationship

HMOs have customer contracts with corporations to ensure medical care for employees and dependents. HMOs also have supply contracts with medical groups and hospitals to deliver the care to these employees. Pricing of the medical care is dependent on volume. An HMO that can deliver volume to a particular provider will likely get preferred pricing. Indeed, HMOs can help direct patients to particular medical providers, through incentives on payment. This arrangement is a very symbiotic relationship for both parties. HMOs can also use these relationships to strengthen customer relationships (something that's badly needed), by using their influence with the providers to increase access to providers for the HMO members and offer better services, such as hiring female OB/GYNs.

pricing. Many of the new partnership supply relationships involve profit sharing, so that win-win results can occur, just as they do with employee relationships based on performance.

Government Relationships. Al Capone recognized the benefit of having good government relationships. Sure, he dealt in an illegal trade and paid off the police, judges, and officials in Chicago—not exactly a business model to replicate. On the other hand, the basic benefit of having and exploiting good government relationships cannot be overstated. Most major businesses and trade associations employ lobbyists and use other communication techniques to ensure that legislators and policy makers hear their points of view.

Government relations can be used to advantage our company or industry or to advantage local companies rather than national. Government rela-

Judo Strategy Applied

Some insurance companies lobbied successfully to increase the capital requirements for certain lines of coverage and, as a result, raised entry barriers to keep new competitors out of the market. Rather than risk competing, they used government relationships to reduce competition, in a display of *judo strategy*.

tions can be used to disadvantage our competitors. In either case, good relationships with regulators, politicians, and government bureaucrats can prove to be very beneficial to business.

Manager's Checklist for Chapter 7

❏ Asset turnover is a key driver of business results.

❏ Looking at each asset category—people, property, and relationships—to identify ideas to improve the use of assets or free up the assets can lead to innovative new strategies.

Judo strategy An approach to competing by avoiding head-to-head contests of strength and, instead, using advantages in speed, agility, and creative thinking to make it difficult for competitors. This recently coined term applies when strategic actions are taken to change the rules of the game.

Getting Close to Government Can Help

Company leaders often have opportunities to recommend someone or volunteer themselves for positions on task forces, commissions, and other advisory bodies. Smart managers participate and become known by the people in government and they and the company gain a reputation as good citizens.

❏ Asset optimization in all categories means better results and more opportunities for growth.

Strategic Thinking: Core Business Analysis

Michael Jordan is arguably the best basketball player of all time. After leaving the University of North Carolina Tar Heels, he began his career in the NBA with the Chicago Bulls in 1984. The early years with the Bulls were lean, but in 1991, 1992, and 1993 the Bulls won consecutive NBA Championship trophies. Jordan, at age 30, felt he had little more to accomplish in professional basketball and he announced his retirement.

But MJ did not really retire. He retired as a basketball player, but retooled his athletic career as a professional baseball player. For about a year and a half, Jordan honed his skills and talents in the minor leagues, working to achieve big league status. But it didn't happen and, on March 18, 1995, Jordan returned to the Bulls with the terse comment, "I'm back!"

The rest is history. Jordan once again led the Bulls to NBA championships in 1996, 1997, and 1998. Then he retired again, in 1999. But again, he returned to the game in 2001, to play two seasons with the Washington Wizards.

Michael Jordan's core business is basketball. When he

focused on those core activities, he succeeded as an individual and as a team player. With Jordan, the Bulls created a dynasty like few others in sports.

Like Jordan, corporations have a core business. In this chapter we explore the meaning of core activities and learn how, by concentrating on our core business, we can find successful strategies for growth and profit.

Core Research

One of the better books on business strategy is *Profit from the Core* by Chris Zook (Harvard Business School Press, 2001). Zook develops a strong case for the notion that truly successful companies have one or at most two core businesses that are well defined and the center of their growth strategy. All of these outstanding companies find extraordinary growth and returns by "sticking to their knitting" in their core business activities. We're going to use the Zook findings as another technique for developing innovative strategies for our own organization.

Zook summarizes his research findings early in the text:

- Most companies that sustain value creation possess only one or two strong cores.
- Private equity companies often achieve their greatest success by buying orphan businesses from diffuse conglomerates, thereby creating focus.
- Spin-offs usually create both focus and value.
- Diversification is associated with lower average valuations than are typical of companies with focused cores.
- The few companies that became smaller and still created value were those that restructured to focus on a strong core, often eventually to grow more vigorously again.[1]

The bottom line here is focus, focus, focus—and if you focus, you'll have a better chance to grow your business.

[1] Chris Zook with James Allen, *Profit from the Core* (Boston: Harvard Business School Press, 2001), p. 24.

Strategic Development Using the Core Business Approach

Our objective is to define a process that we can use to determine strategic options for our company. Here we're going to use the concept of the core business to find new strategies to grow and improve our business. Frankly, the process we'll use is very easy, consisting of the following steps:

- Define the core clearly.
- Detail those activities that lie outside the core.
- Use value chain analysis to find new strategies that deepen our focus on the core business.
- Prioritize the most promising strategies and estimate the impact of each.
- Contemplate the divestment of activities that lie outside the core.

In order to effectively use this process for strategic innovation, an organization should assemble a team of managers from different disciplines and levels to determine the assessment, investigate the alternatives, and make recommendations. Throughout the process, senior management needs to monitor and support the progress of the team.

Defining the Core

According to Zook, and common sense, a company's core business is defined by that set of products, customer segments, processes, and technologies in which you can build the greatest competitive advantage. Two things to note here: first, the core is defined by the decisions that a company makes about its business model, and second, we may not have yet realized the competitive advantage positioning in our core business, and that's why investigating our core can lead to better strategies.

Defining the core usually means narrowing our focus. It requires examining our portfolio of products to find those that are the strongest in their markets. It requires studying our target customers to determine in which markets we're best. It requires looking at our processes and technologies to establish where we can sustain an edge on our competition.

Lets take a look at Coca-Cola. Here's a company, started in 1886, that has focused upon its core business, soft drinks. For about 100 years, it was all about Coke, the original drink. In the 1980s, however, the company recognized the emerging calorie-consciousness of the consumer and introduced Diet Coke. The product was a huge and immediate success. Shortly thereafter, Coca-Cola, worried about the sustainability of its taste, decided to change the formulation of Coke. After substantial taste testing, New Coke was born and marketed. But the market responded that it preferred the old Coke, which the company quickly brought back as Classic Coke. For a while, it offered both. Today there's only one Coke. In order to grow their business, the company expanded its product offerings, but only in its core business, soft drinks. Over time Coca-Cola augmented its brand lineup substantially with Sprite, Barq's, Hi-C, and Nestea, among others. Today Coca-Cola markets over 300 brands in 200 countries. The most recent addition was Dassani water. The company recognized that bottled water is a soft drink in great demand, so, using its great resources (machine and store distribution, bottling dominance, and market power) it could enter the market in a big way.

The story of Coca-Cola is that of a company that's focused on its market (soft drinks) and its customers' changing tastes and needs and that uses its assets to support its core business and core brands. Coca-Cola is also the story of a successful company that has grown by exploiting its core business almost single-mindedly.

So how do we define our core business? Zook suggests that we look to those areas in which we have a clear, strong competitive advantage. If this sounds familiar, it is. Go back to our SWOT analysis and concentrate on strengths. There should be a list of five to 10 items based on results, environmental analysis, customer analysis, and our internal audit that define the power of the company. Our core business is defined by our strengths. Use the list from SWOT to help define the core business.

The core business discussion can be difficult, because many companies have, over time, migrated to operating a number of businesses. One way to come to a conclusion about the core is to do an exercise. Gather a group of key individuals from all areas of the organization for a two-hour meeting. Pose the following question:

> If we were forced to sell off *all* of our businesses except
> for one, which one would we keep?

The idea here is to force us to think about the business at which we're really good and in which we have strength in the marketplace. It may be necessary to use a facilitator in this discussion, because turf issues become visible very quickly. Yet it's important to have a broad representation in the discussion, so that you can achieve a level of consensus—or at least resignation. Now, of course, we're not going to sell all of our businesses, but the exercise leads us to the core.

Identifying the core business is just the beginning to finding new strategies for growth and profit. The idea is that, by focusing on the core business exclusively, we can find growth and profit that we miss by being distracted with other business lines that do not leverage our power in the core business.

Southwest True to the Core

Southwest Airlines is a good role model. Their core business is short haul, low priced, air transportation. Southwest has not dabbled in international flights or in high-service segments, like first class. By persistently pounding that market with focus, the airline is the jewel of the industry.

When managers are asked to look for growth ideas, it's natural to imagine new products or new services or making acquisitions, yet the core business experience and approach suggests that if we relentlessly look at our key current markets and products with the most advantage, we can find growth that we might overlook by getting into new businesses.

Harley Makes Bikes

Harley Davidson makes motorcycles. They know their markets, have a tremendous brand, and operate with efficiency and quality. And essentially that's all they do. Harley has withstood the challenge by Japanese cycle makers and has grown its market throughout the business cycle. Now Harley markets and promotes other products, but the absolute key factor here is that these efforts support the core business of selling motorcycles and are not considered as independent of the motorcycle business.

Working the Core

Once we've identified our core business, we want to work it exhaustively. There are five steps to achieving this goal:

- Evaluate the core business markets in depth.
- Deliver excellence in the operation of the core business.
- Explore the financial performance potential without anything new.
- Penetrate the market deeply.
- Look to adjacencies.

By taking these five steps, in order, a strategy for profitable growth can emerge that is linked to our most powerful competitive advantages.

Evaluate the Core Markets

In order to find growth in existing businesses, we need to know the markets in detail. One tool that helps us accomplish this task is the competitor/segment matrix. This device lets us see the core market in depth, and discover where the opportunities for profitable growth may lie. It is a simple tool, but

Adjacency A business idea that permits a company to extend the boundaries of its core business, using and even reinforcing the strength of the core business. So adjacencies expand the core, but remain core business activities.

According to Zook, "What distinguishes an adjacency from another growth opportunity is the extent to which it draws on the customer relationships, technologies, or skills in the core business to build competitive advantage in a new adjacent competitive arena."

Business Changes to Travel

Zook provides an excellent example of an adjacency. The original business of American Express was the money order. It was a fabulous success. But the company couldn't make the product work in Europe, so in 1891 it invented a modification of the product called the *traveler's cheque*. The rest, as they say, is history.

requires some research to construct. Figure 8-1 shows a sample of imaginary data for a brewery to illustrate the point.

First, we identify the competitors. It's best to list them all along with revenues and trends. Second, we identify the market segments. This step is particularly important because different segments usually require different approaches and features. By identifying the segments and their revenue and growth, we can see opportunities for our core business.

In the simple example of Figure 8-1, the segments are the various customer groupings that tend to share the same buying process, needs, and service levels. In the case of selling beer, "Retail, Large" means the grocery chains, big box stores (like Sam's Club), and other large stores that sell to individual customers. "Retail, Small" represents outlets like convenience stores, liquor stores, and small, individual grocery merchants. Restaurants are an obvious customer segment that mixes bottled

What About GE?

All of this talk about focusing on the core and the success that companies following the approach enjoy begs the question: What about GE? General Electric certainly is one of the most successful companies over the last 20 years and it doesn't seem to operate with just one core business.

The key is that each of GE's business units is operated as its own core unit. Whether it's aircraft engines or appliances, GE business units are core businesses in themselves. The overriding operating philosophy of GE corporate management that ties the portfolio together is the mantra that each business must be number one or two in its market, as former president Jack Welch mandated. This keeps the business unit leaders focused on their execution and their core business.

Competitors	Segments				
	Retail Large	Retail Small	Restaurants	Taverns	Total
Us	$120	$90 ↑	$40	$150 ↓	$400
A	$200 ↓	$120	$60	$80	$460
B	$50	$75 ↑			$125
C	$40	$10	$140 ↓	$120	$310
Total	$500	$320	$280	$400	$1,500/ $1,295

Historic Growth	+2%	+5%	+8%	−4%	+4%
Forecast Growth	+8%	+6%	+10%	+2%	+7%
Our Margin	+12%	+19%	+14%	+15%	+17%

Figure 8-1. Competitor/segment matrix

and bulk (keg) products. And, of course, taverns also buy both bulk and bottled goods.

The numbers in the boxes provide the revenue by competitor and customer segment. Arrows, either up or down, indicate any meaningful trend in the market for a company. Each company's total revenue is summed in the last column. Each segment's total size is summed in the last row.

At the bottom of the page is a matrix that provides growth rates and margins. For each segment, the historic (past three years) growth rate is entered in the first row. The second row is the estimate of the estimated growth of each segment. The final row reports the typical margin that we enjoy in each segment and for the business as a whole.

The great thing about constructing this analysis is that on one page we can see the market and the opportunities for our core business. A couple of examples from the sample page will give a flavor for the potential. We see that our large competitor 'A' is trending down in the large retail segment, which is a growth segment. If we can figure out why, then this is an attractive source of growth, even though our margins have been moderate there. Also our restaurant business has been weak on the top line. With a good growth forecast and specialty beer company 'C' having trouble, we may have a brand that can score big.

The point of this exercise is twofold:

- We understand the trends, opportunities, and competition in our markets.
- We focus on customer segments and their individual needs to determine how we might penetrate better, and beat the competitors.

From this single page, we can test all proposed strategies by looking at the facts in the marketplace.

Deliver Excellence in the Operation of the Core Business

Before we can find the best strategies for our core business, we should ensure that the business runs like a well-oiled machine in every respect. Chances are that it doesn't! By putting an absolute emphasis on the core business, with no distractions and no excuses, managers can find efficiencies, process improvements, and marketing insights that may have been overlooked in the past.

Operational excellence means working to achieve benchmarks in all components of the value chain. To some companies, this has meant product quality and efficiency, but for the core business approach to work we must go beyond those issues. Excellence means looking closely at our customers, by segment, and understanding what factors contribute to their complete satisfaction. The focus that this approach requires is that of a new business or a turnaround situation, a sense that there is burning platform that we must work hard and fast to fix. And it's important to note that new businesses are being formed

Take a Cue from GE

Smart Managing

General Electric has been very successful and it does many things well. But it wasn't always that way. Jack Welch, the former CEO of the company, made some very important operational changes with the goal of being number one or two in each market. Two examples are Workout and Six Sigma.

Welch inherited a company that was very complex and bureaucratic. He initiated Workout, a program in which employees identified things that were keeping them from doing their jobs more easily, faster, less expensively, and better. As a result of Workout, GE became a streamlined and much improved organization.

Welch also recognized the cost of mistakes and rework, particularly on big items like power plants and aircraft engines. To fix this problem, GE fully adopted the concept of Six Sigma. In short, Six Sigma is a method of using hard data and statistical analysis to make all business processes work perfectly the first time. As a result, costs go down and margins go up. Few companies have been so completely aligned with the Six Sigma philosophy as GE, but the results speak for themselves.

as specialists every day, with the sole intent of finding the weakness of the market players and exploiting it.

One useful tool is called *fault-tree analysis*. It's commonly used in accident situations to fully understand what factors contributed to a loss and how we might engineer or operate to prevent future losses. For example, the National Transportation Safety Board uses fault-tree analysis every time a commercial airplane crashes and NASA used it to investigate the shuttle Columbia disaster in January 2003.

Decompose Customer Satisfaction

TOOLS

Fault-tree analysis is a deductive, top-down method of analyzing a situation or a system. It involves identifying all of the factors in the situation or the system that could cause the event in question.

Fault trees allow for a graphic representation of the factors that contribute to the event, using symbols. Then you ask questions, including the following key questions:

• What could go wrong and cause a problem?
• What would be the consequences?

The technique of fault-tree analysis is simple. Ask the question "Why?" over and over again, until you've completely uncovered the contributing factors. So let's use a modified fault-tree analysis to find the causes of customer satisfaction and dissatisfaction.

Figure 8-2 provides a simple look at what decomposition might look like. Every business and every market segment are different; so we need to apply the technique many times, but the ideas remain consistent.

The basic question is "Why are customers satisfied?" If, as in Figure 8-2, the answer is four factors—price, quality, service quality, and delivery—then we ask "Why?" again: Why does price satisfy? Why does quality satisfy? Why does service quality satisfy? Why does delivery satisfy? We continue to ask until we cannot break down the components any further. Through this exercise, we can determine the strengths and missed opportunities in our operating and selling.

By focusing on our identified core business, we can and should improve operational excellence, because we're focusing all of our management attention to this mission.

Explore the Financial Performance Potential Without Anything New

Suppose senior management of the organization tells the business unit managers of the core business, "Show me what this business can do with nothing new—no new products and no acquisitions. And I want to see a business plan next week including projected financials for the next three years." The business unit management is forced to focus on the existing business and squeeze every bit of growth and profit from its product line, business model, and distribution system.

In essence, that is what focusing on the core challenges managers to do. It makes us sharpen our pencils, drive efficiencies, and know the customer like we've never done before. Observers, like Zook, have found if we do this, it's amazing what new revenue and profitability we're able to find.

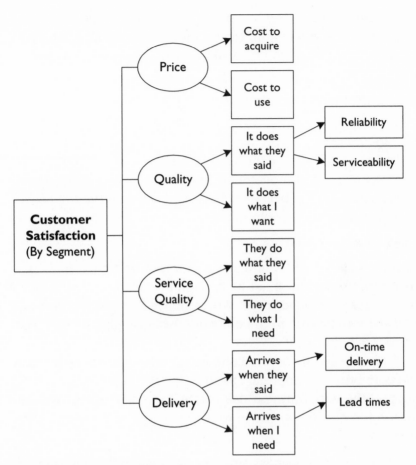

Figure 8-2. Decomposition of customer satisfaction

Of course, good managers don't accept the projected results on the first pass. Good managers push for more, and often there's more to be found than first meets the eye. Managers frequently underestimate the size of their markets and overestimate their share. If this is true, the focused discipline of the core approach will find innovative ways within the current business model to add revenue and returns.

Suppose that we use the "nothing new" framework and the results show that we can meet financial and business goals without anything new! Wouldn't that be delightful? New products, new markets, and acquisitions are all very expensive and risky ventures. Sticking to the existing business but making it better is less risky and obviously easier, since we know the value chain so well.

Penetrate the Market Deeply

In this step we execute: we gain market share in segments that we already serve. To do this, we look to current, previous, and potential customers for the growth that we seek. Through our analysis and the improvements in operations that we've made, we've identified the best and most opportunistic market segments and competitors to attack.

Look to Adjacencies

In some cases, just hammering at our new and improved current core business will not be enough to meet our objectives. In these cases, we need more. Where do we find new things to do and still remain true to the one core business philosophy? The answer is adjacencies.

There's one major condition for an adjacency to be valid in the core business approach to strategy: the adjacency must support the core business. We can test the adjacencies with at least three questions, one of which needs to be answered affirmatively.

- Is the core business stronger because of the adjacent business?
- Does the adjacent business add value for the core customers?
- Can the adjacent business help defend against attacks on the core by competitors?

The adjacent business must benefit the core business in order to be considered a valid business idea to pursue.

There are six categories of adjacencies:

- new geographies
- new channels
- new customer segments

- new products
- new value chain steps
- new businesses

We'll devote the rest of this chapter to discussing these categories of adjacencies.

New Geographies. Geographical expansion is probably the easiest type of adjacent move for a business. Opportunities to bring existing products to new geographical markets can lead to substantial growth and profit.

For example, copying one successful Italian restaurant by building another in a new geography not only provides growth through the new location, but also builds the brand of the original. The example of Culver's expansion, as discussed in Chapters 2 and 5, is classic geographical expansion and support for the core.

Today's world invites global expansion as a business opportunity. In order for geographical expansion, whether global or local, to be a valid course for core growth, the new location cannot be a distraction from the core business. If regulations, language, brand distortion, or other factors make the international expansion problematic for the business operators, then it's a bad idea and we should look to other adjacencies.

New Channels. How do our goods and services get to their customers? That's the essential issue in dealing with channels of distribution. The current structure of our core business uses one or more channels to deliver our goods and services. When we change or add channels in order to drive growth, that's an adjacency strategy.

The whole point of adding a channel is to sell more products. Sometimes, however, if we add a channel of distribution, we actually can do the opposite. Channel conflict—the turf war between elements of different channels—can hurt our efforts in two ways. First, channel members may retaliate against the company for opening a new channel by sending current customers to our competitors. Two, distraction of the sales effort in both new and

Changing Channels

Grocery stores sell cereal, among many other things. So most grocery stores were very unhappy with companies like General Mills and Quaker Oats when these companies decided to sell their products (Cheerios, Instant Oatmeal, and others) through warehouse stores, companies like Costco and Sam's Club. Without the warehouse stores, the only large outlet for these cereal items was grocery stores. When General Mills opened the warehouse channel to some of its best brands, grocery stores no longer enjoyed exclusivity and, therefore, lost some appeal for shoppers. But because the growth of warehouse stores has been great, the cereal manufacturers felt that they could not ignore that channel, so they went ahead.

old channels may undermine performance in each.

Channels can make a huge difference to your business in terms of opening up growth opportunities. Here's an example.

There's a decorative stone company in Minnesota that owns a few quarries. Traditionally, it sold these building materials through representatives working with construction companies. However, when the company began to market its products to architects, business took off. Now, when architects design properties, they specify this company's specific rock brand in the blueprints and competitors get cut out even from a bidding process.

The newest new channel is the Internet. Probably more has been written and tried on the topic of e-commerce than any subject in the last 10 years. Many Internet channels have been successful: banking and financial services companies, eBay, travel services, and music and books. Other attempts have failed. Many companies thought that the Internet channel required little maintenance, management, and attention; they were wrong. Like all channels, the Internet requires support and, as an adjacency, needs to be supportive of the core business.

New Customer Segments. The more we learn about our current customer segments and buying behaviors, the more new opportunities become visible. One opportunity is to see segments within segments.

Colleges and universities, for example, traditionally target the education needs of the 17- to 22-year-old age group. But a little market research indicated that adults of all ages are interested in lifelong learning. By altering the marketing of courses, particularly with respect to the times of when the courses are offered, these organizations expanded their market greatly;

> **Channel Conflict** **⚠ CAUTION! ⚠**
>
> There may be no way to eliminate the problems of channel conflict, especially with the growth of the Web as a marketing channel. That channel is raising problems for companies everywhere.
>
> If you don't sell online, how will that affect your sales? Can you ignore the adjacency that your competitors are likely using? But if you sell online, how will that affect your conventional distributors and dealers? It's essential to have a plan for minimizing the problems of channel conflict for the Web.

almost all colleges now offer programs for lifetime learning opportunities. In fact, one of the great success and expansion stories of the last few years is the University of Phoenix. This for-profit university specializes in educational programming, both degree and non-degree, to non-traditional students, mostly working adults and mid-career retooling. Programs are designed to meet the needs of this segment almost exclusively, using both traditional and online approaches. The success of the University of Phoenix highlights the fact that traditional colleges and universities were neglecting this customer segment; the University of Phoenix devised strategies to meet the needs of that segment and has grown greatly.

New Products. While it's good to think big, when it comes to new products there's a lot of benefit, in most situations, to thinking small and/or incrementally. Remember that the main idea of the core business approach to building business strategy is that there are plenty of growth and profit opportunities if we concentrate on our core. So for new products, the core approach is to explore three types of new products:

- next-generation products

> **⚠ CAUTION!**
>
> ### Make the Core Business Sexy
>
> Innovation is exciting. People are generally drawn to the latest new thing. But since failure rates of new-to-the-world products are so high, we must be careful not to suck all the oxygen out of the core business room by building a new addition to the house. Good managers are passionate about the core business and can find innovation and growth in the existing product lines by keeping the entire organization energized by the promise of growth in the core areas. A positive attitude is the first ingredient in the recipe for growth—and that starts with management. Even subtle negative remarks, jokes, or body language can have a devastating effect on the morale of staff working to find growth in the core lines.

- support services
- complementary products

New-to-the-world products should be considered, but after exploring these other areas that are closer to the core.

Next-Generation Products. "New and improved" has been a standard approach to promoting products since marketing began. Next-generation products are simply the new and improved versions of existing products. The next generation evolves principally for two reasons: defense and offense.

On defense, our competitors target our deficiencies or their differentiating factors. As they take market share from us, one response is to redesign our product so its benefits better meet consumer needs. By updating our products, we defend our market position.

For example, when one wireless telephone service provider adds an improvement (like including nationwide long-distance), the others follow quickly. This is a defensive response, to retain share in the face of competitor actions.

On offense, we look to capture more market share by changing the product to appeal to a wider or potentially different customer segment. Sometimes we target weak competitors; sometimes we target unmet customer needs. In any event, we redesign or repackage our product to generate new business outside of our current customers.

In almost any consumer products category, we have seen a proliferation of designed to gain a wider appeal, but linked to an existing product brand. For two examples, look at toothpaste and golf balls. In toothpaste, it used to be Crest versus Colgate. Now each brand has about five products (whitening, breath freshening, tartar control, etc.) and at least a couple of packaging options. These new products target other competitors (Rembrandt for whitening and Aquafresh for breath freshening, for instance), while new packaging attempts to take share from any competitor only using the original tube packaging. In golf balls it's the same story. Now there are balls that are specialized: distance, accuracy, soft feel, more spin, and combinations of these properties. Rather than replacing existing products, golf ball manufacturers have continued to add new lines to broaden the appeal of their brand to many segments.

Support Services. Selling services to support the company's products may provide a growth business that strengthens the core product business. Mr. Goodwrench is a brand that General Motors began years ago to promote vehicle service in its dealerships. By branding the service concept, implying quality and honesty (for example, they used the phase "using genuine GM parts"), GM tried to recapture some business lost to independent gas stations and freestanding service centers. Recently, however, GM has opened freestanding Mr. Goodwrench service centers. Here the strategy is to compete with Jiffy Lube and other companies for simple maintenance and to generate new revenue growth.

Service can be big business. In looking at the opportunities to add revenue and profit through new products, service initiatives can provide excellent possibilities. But we need not think of service only as maintenance or repair. Service offerings also exist at the buying, delivery, use, and disposal phases of the buying process, as outlined in Chapter 1.

A few examples are instructive. Insurance companies traditionally require buyers to pay their entire premium in a lump sum. Insurers found, however, that they could finance the premiums in installments and charge a fee to do so, therefore creating a new revenue stream. Many Internet and mail order houses have found that delivery options can generate incremental revenue and profit. By offering overnight, two-day, or standard delivery options, these firms could charge fees well in excess of the costs of their delivery expenses and satisfy the customers' needs for immediate delivery as well. Banks have learned that ATM fees are a valuable new revenue stream. As customers use ATMs more, the fees associated with electronic and convenient access to cash and banking services have become a significant part of the banks' cash flows. Some appliance stores have found that by providing for disposal of old appliances, they could be more attractive than competitors and charge higher prices for this value-added service.

Notice that all of these service options pass the adjacency test questions about supporting the core business. Core customers are more satisfied, and strengthened relations with customers help companies defend better against their competitors.

Complementary Products. One way to find new products is to look for items that our customers will tend also to purchase. Complementary products support the core business and can generate significant income. We've already mentioned one example: Harley-Davidson sells a line of merchandise related to its cycles—accessories, apparel, beverage items (mugs, glasses, bottle openers), and products to commemorate its 100th anniversary.

Here's another example. Barnes and Noble Bookstores know their customers. By and large, people who frequent bookstores like to read and reading is a leisurely pursuit. Why not put a coffee shop in the store, so people can linger and purchase coffee and snacks while they peruse the books? Readers tend to like music, so they sell CDs. Readers also like to write, so offer greeting cards, journals, and writing tools. All these examples are complementary products, like salted snacks are complements to beer.

New Value Chain Steps. Once we define our core business and our value chain, we can evaluate any opportunities for growth

> ### Big Money for College Sports
> Major universities with big-time athletic departments face many financial challenges. In general, state support for public universities is dwindling and only a few sports can generate enough ticket revenue to carry their own weight. One way to find revenue and growth opportunities lies in licensing apparel and related goods. Whenever you buy a T-shirt or cap with a university logo, the manufacturer or seller of the product must pay a licensing fee to the university for use of the mark. Universities are not in the clothing business, but they know the popularity of these soft items that complement the sporting activities and provide considerable revenue. And they clearly support the core business.

along the value chain. One way to see adjacencies along the value chain is to look backward, toward manufacturing and supply of raw goods, or forward, toward distribution and sales.

The airlines have made a big move forward with huge investments in direct selling and Internet distribution of e-tickets. Sears moved backward along the value chain by acquiring Lands' End, the clothing and soft goods supplier. Each of these maneuvers is an attempt to support the core business by finding profitable growth in new activities related to the core.

Sears, for example, had created two very strong brands in Craftsman tools and Kenmore appliances. All the market research indicates that these two brands are solid attractors for customers to Sears stores. For years, however, Sears has tried to find some magic in its clothing lines without much success. The acquisition of Lands' End was intended to immediately add a strong brand and more traffic and sales in the stores. One question remains, however: will traditional Lands' End customers abandon the brand and go to Eddie Bauer or L.L. Bean, because of the acquisition by Sears?

New Businesses. Here's a good question: Is it possible to find a new business outside of our core that supports our core business? The answer is yes.

Look at Disney. By creating lovable and lasting characters—first with cartoons, then in movies and television—the company

> **⚠ CAUTION!**
>
> ### Value Chain Hazards
>
> Whether we move up or down the value chain looking for new opportunities to generate revenue or cost savings, there are dangers lurking in this approach. Producers and sellers both are very cautious about doing business with their competitors.
>
> Take the case of PepsiCo acquiring Pizza Hut. Pepsi certainly gained the fountain drink concession (its core business) in the Pizza Hut stores. But Pepsi also lost many opportunities to offer its drink items in every other pizza store because of its investment in Pizza Hut. This factor, and the related issues of operating businesses outside the core (restaurants are not just the drinks business), led PepsiCo to divest itself of Pizza Hut, KFC, and Taco Bell in 1997, creating Tricon Global Restaurants (now Yum! Brands).

expanded into theme parks, retail stores, and even a hockey team (Anaheim's Mighty Ducks). The key is to find those businesses that core customers continue to support with an ever-increasing amount of their resources. Every time a child first watches *Snow White* or *The Jungle Book* on video, Disney is ready with action figures, licensed soft goods, and a theme park or two to continue that child's love affair with the characters in the story. Since the operations of theme parks and movie studios and retail stores are quite different, it's absolutely critical that these businesses are linked by the vision of the company and a group of common, well-defined customers.

The new business approach to growing the core is difficult. Again Disney provides a good example, since the company has invested in many businesses that were not sustainable, such as Capital Cities/ABC. Clearly, there must be strong core competency or customer relationships involved; otherwise, the move into new businesses would be diversification, which is almost the antithesis of the core business approach.

Defining our core business and looking to strengthen it through focus and smart adjacencies can be a very powerful method for finding business strategies. By using the process outlined here, managers can find new, profitable opportunities for growth.

Close, But Not Close Enough

A business that's similar or related is not necessarily an adjacency. Here's a prime example.

Quaker Oats bought Snapple in 1993 for $1.7 billion. In 1997, Quaker sold Snapple for $300 million. No one has ever said, "Buy high and sell low"! Quaker thought that the Snapple business would be great because it complemented the Quaker Gatorade brand in the drink market. The strategy failed for a variety of reasons, which are detailed well in an article by John Deighton ("How Snapple Got Its Juice Back," *Harvard Business Review,* January 2002). The point is simple. Just because a business is attractive and is in the same product category as our own does not mean that it will pass the core business tests that we've outlined here.

Two footnotes: in 2000, Quaker became a division of PepsiCo and the company that bought Snapple from Quaker sold the drink to Cadbury Schweppes ... for about $1 billion.

Manager's Checklist for Chapter 8

❑ Products, competencies, customer segments, processes, and/or technology that provide our organization with the best competitive advantage define the core business.

❑ Companies that have only one or, at most, two core businesses have been more successful over the long term than firms with a wider business scope.

❑ Find your core by asking, "If we were forced to sell all of our activities but one, what would we keep?"

❑ Operational excellence is a key ingredient to core success.

❑ Adjacencies can provide excellent profitable growth potential, but only if they pass the core business tests:

- Is the core business stronger because of the adjacent business?
- Does the adjacent business add value for the core customers?
- Can the adjacent business help defend against attacks on the core by competitors?

Strategic Thinking: Ten Tested Business Strategies

Imitation is the highest form of flattery.

Those who fail to learn the lessons of history are bound to repeat its mistakes.

Why reinvent the wheel?

There's nothing new under the sun.

Get the point? Whatever you're dealing with in your business or, for that matter, in your personal life, somebody has probably dealt with it in the past. Why not borrow from the past and adopt the lessons of history for yourself?

Well, let's apply this thinking to developing a strategy for our business. In this chapter, we review 10 successful business strategies from the past 100 years and suggest that maybe one or more are right for your business. If so, go ahead and steal the idea. This brand of innovation does not lie in the newness of the idea, but rather in the newness of the application.

Background

In an article in the business journal, *Strategy + Business* (Vol. 23, Second Quarter 2001), "Top 10 Innovation Themes," David Y. Choi and Liisa Valikangas purported to identify the 10 essential strategic innovation themes that are repeated and proven successful over time. They distilled the list from nearly 200 strategies over the past century. These themes or strategic ideas are far ranging and provide a good checklist for finding opportunities for our business. Here are those top 10:

1. Consolidation: rolling up a fragmented industry
2. Bypassing: cutting out the intermediaries
3. Value Migration: shifting to a related but more profitable niche
4. Teaming Up: creating alliances with suppliers
5. Digital Delivery: providing Internet-based business activities
6. Deep Connections: appealing to emotional attachments with a brand
7. ASAP: delivering products or information faster
8. Customization: letting customers design the end product to their specs
9. Mass-Market: extending availability of products to broad markets
10. Fix-It-for-Me: solving the customer's problem with a breakthrough solution

In each case, we need to assess our circumstances, understand our markets, and test the application of these ideas for our company.

Consolidation

Consolidation has been a remarkably successful strategy for firms in a fragmented industry that have opportunities to improve their revenue-generating power or cost experience by getting larger. A consolidator uses capital to acquire the small

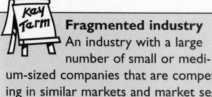

players, creating a larger and hopefully more powerful competitor.

The classic case was the growth of Standard Oil in the late 19th century. John D. Rockefeller founded the company with his brother in 1866 and then acquired many small oil companies, creating a giant firm, which by 1879 was doing about 90% of the refining in the U.S. and which over time has morphed into Exxon-Mobil, one of the world's largest companies.

Banks have also been engaged as consolidators. In almost every community, there are a few large national banking companies, like Bank One, U.S. Bank, and Bank of America. These banks have grown by acquiring local or regional banks and then bringing them into the larger organization, under a single brand.

The keys to a successful consolidation strategy are in identifying that many small players are available and then that acquiring and integrating these businesses into a single platform can lead to synergies. A consolidation or roll-up strategy relies on the notion that the combined company can do more or better than a multitude of smaller ones. Clearly by having more volume a firm can negotiate better supplier contracts and may generate more revenue through expansion into new geographies.

M&A 101

Suppose we find a publicly traded company that we want to acquire. The stock is currently at $10 a share. If we offer $10 a share to buy the company, our offer would be rejected relatively quickly, since there's no benefit to the shareholders to sell (unless they know the stock price is going down!). So we must offer more in order to get all of the shareholders to sell. If we offer $14 a share, a 40% premium, we might have a chance to get all of the stock. But to make our investment pay off, we must find that extra $4 per share, and more, in synergies, through increasing revenue, lowering costs, and/or lowering risk by combining the firms. Knowing the potential for synergies, of course, is the best way to offer a price that satisfies the sellers and gives us an opportunity to earn a reasonable return on our investment.

Smart Managing

Finding synergies is absolutely critical to any acquisition, whether in a roll-up or simply a one-off deal. The reason is simple. In the majority of acquisitions, the buyer pays more than the target company is worth as a stand-alone organization. The difference between the price paid and the value of the company is called the *acquisition premium*. Premiums usually range between 20% and 60% of the purchase price. The managers of a company that pay more than a target company is worth must see some hidden benefit in the combination, some change in operating results that the target company could not find on its own. Otherwise, the buyer would never receive an adequate return on the investment made in the purchase.

History reveals that industry consolidation can be a very successful strategy for organizations that have the capital and risk tolerance to execute this approach. One good example of an industry roll-up is taking place now, in the consolidation of the insurance agency business. Thousands of small, local, independent insurance agencies have existed in the commercial landscape of the country. Each agency represents certain insurance companies and sells to a local market. Each agency maintains the comprehensive sales, administrative, and claims systems to operate its business. Enter a company like Brown & Brown, Inc. of Daytona Beach, Florida. Management sees at

least two opportunities for cost and revenue synergies in con-
solidating this industry. One, in combining the systems into a
consolidated back office, there are cost savings and the staff of
the local agency is freed up to sell more. Two, by capturing
more volume, the bigger company can negotiate better deals
with the insurance companies it represents and thus generate
more commission revenue.

The results of Brown & Brown's strategy are very clear. In
1999, the company had total revenue of $176.4 million; at the
end of 2002, total revenue for the year reached $455.7 million.
This increase in revenue is a 37.2% annual compound growth
rate for the three-year period. In 2001 alone, the company did
26 acquisitions of smaller agencies. As an important side note,
another realized benefit of this strategy has been to bring into
Brown & Brown new, experienced, and talented insurance personnel to manage the organization and provide insurance sales
expertise. In executing this strategy, Brown & Brown has
become the sixth largest independent insurance intermediary in
the U.S. To find out more about the Brown & Brown story, go to
the Web site at www.bbinsurance.com.

Bypassing

Another strategy that has been very effective in delivering
excellent results for some firms is bypassing. In this approach,
firms carefully analyze their value chain and then find steps that
can be eliminated to create more value for the customers and
the business. Bypassing is particularly prevalent in the area of
distribution.

Probably the best contemporary example of the bypassing
strategy is from Dell Computer. Michael Dell, founder of the
company, made the decision at the beginning to offer computers
direct to the public and bypass distribution through all the retail
outlets. His idea was to build computers to order, as the orders
came into Dell directly from the end users. When an order came
in, Dell would collect the purchase price via credit card, then
make the machine and ship it directly to the customer.

By skipping the retail distributors, Dell achieved a number of benefits, some possibly unanticipated. First, Dell satisfies an unmet need by letting the buyer choose the specifications of the computer, designing the system rather than buying off the shelf or from a retailer's inventory. Second, because Dell makes the computers to order and since computer parts are in plentiful supply, Dell's order cycle for parts is very short and parts inventory is low, which reduces carrying costs. Third, since prices on technology parts tend to go down over time and new technology (for example, processor speed) comes to market often, Dell can offer the latest technology before his competitors, who have to reduce the stocks of old inventory first before building with the latest version of the chips. Fourth, since Dell has the money before delivering the product, Dell's cash flow is positive, while competitors have negative cash flows. Put all of these benefits together and Dell also has the advantage of being able to price its computers extremely competitively.

Dell was founded in 1984. By 2000 Dell led the computer industry in market share. Sales over the last four quarters were $35 billion. And what has happened to Dell's competitors? Compaq and Hewlett-Packard merged, IBM moved to direct selling of PCs, and a host of other companies have fallen by the wayside. If you look at the Dell Web site, www.dell.com, the role of "going direct," bypassing, is the dominant theme and the foundation of its business model.

The Internet creates an entirely new distribution approach for many businesses, and the bypassing strategy is truly in vogue for 21st-century businesses. Charles Schwab and E-Trade have adopted a bypassing strategy for those customers looking to avoid stockbrokers. Amazon provides access to books and music (among other things) exclusively through online purchasing.

Lands' End's direct marketing approach to traditional clothing has been a success, so much so that Sears acquired Lands' End in 2002. It will be interesting to watch Sears manage these assets over time.

To see if bypassing can work for our company, we must understand our value chain and determine whether any links of the chain can be skipped or done differently. In looking at those steps, we must then determine whether we or our customers can realize any benefits because of the proposed changes.

Value Migration

The strategy of value migration is the technique of leveraging some aspect of your business (products, expertise, customers) into a new, related area to create value. The strategy is particularly useful as returns diminish or as growth slows in the core area of your business. As a result, we look to find new ways to garner customers, sales, or margins.

A good example of the value migration strategy is Citigroup, the large financial services company, formed in 1998 through a merger of Citibank and the Travelers Group. Travelers, headed by Sanford Weill, was well known as a leading multi-line insurance company. Over the course of the 1980s, Weill acquired a number of companies in the financial services industry to add to the insurance base of Travelers. These companies included Primerica, a financial services marketing company, and Smith Barney, the large brokerage and investment bank. These acquisitions began a tradition of value migration in the company.

Since each firm was centered in the financial services arena, the opportunities to cross-sell products to individual and corporate clients created new channels for additional revenue and greater profits. The mega-merger between Citibank and Travelers continued the value migration theme. Citibank, one of the world's largest banks, and its customers now had access to the investment products at Smith Barney and the insurance products and distribution of Travelers and Primerica. Also, Travelers, Primerica, and Smith Barney could leverage the products, services, and expertise of Citibank. For example, now an investment client at Smith Barney could get a mortgage from Citibank or a corporate borrower of Citibank could access the underwriting, research, and trading services of Smith

> ### Understand the Value of Brands
> An interesting aspect of the Citigroup approach to value
> migration is that each of the companies has retained its
> own brand identity. The brands are linked together with the "Citigroup"
> tag line and the red umbrella logo. By retaining the company names,
> images, and brands, Citigroup believes that it can keep customers iden-
> tifying with the merged companies and maintain their loyalty. Other
> firms have taken a different branding approach, in which all the names
> and brands have been given up to a single brand, either existing or new.

Barney. The end result has been a powerhouse financial services
company.

Recent events, however, in the wake of the corporate scandals of 2002 have put a damper on the convergence of the
financial services area; particularly hard hit are the relationships
between banking and investment banking services. Citigroup
will have to weave its way through the maze of new realities in
order to keep its business model vibrant. Citigroup also has recognized that the link between property and liability insurance
and other financial services is not as robust as it might have
expected; in 2002 the company spun off Travelers Property
Casualty Corporation in an IPO. Notice that market realities and
environmental changes require that strategies be flexible and
firms need to regularly assess their situation.

For a different model of value migration, we turn to
Walgreens. Historically a drug store, Walgreens has used the
value migration strategy to change the nature of its stores and
the results of its business. Walk into any Walgreens and you will
find, in addition to a drug store, a convenience store (bread,
milk, snack items), a card store, a cosmetic counter, a mini
hardware store with seasonal items, and a complete photo
shop. In fact the photo shop has become a dominant feature in
the stores, offering all photo accessories (film, batteries, single-
use cameras), one-hour processing, and digital processing of
prints and enlargements. In all these cases, Walgreens is using
its customers' need for convenience to offer new products and
services and expecting that the traffic will also lead to additional

sales of traditional items. So is Walgreens still a drug store? The answer is probably yes, because we don't know what else to call it, yet the value migration strategy has led to a 10-year revenue growth from $7.5 billion to $28.7 billion and an earnings growth from $220 million in 1992 to $1 billion in 2002.

Teaming Up

Sometimes we just can't do it all. Sometimes if we let a specialist do it, the results are better. That's the essence of teaming up as a strategic option. In teaming up, businesses become partners or allies with their suppliers, and usually forgo a more vertically integrated approach. With teaming up, a firm does not have to own assets, processes, or institutions in order to use them effectively. In a way, teaming up is an acquisition strategy, looking for synergies between firms, but without the acquisition!

In 2003 Toyota Motors introduced a new vehicle called the Matrix. The Matrix is geared to a young buyer: reasonably low priced, versatile interior configurations, funky styling, and good mileage. At GM, the Pontiac Division also introduced a new model, the Vibe. Styled slightly differently from the Matrix, more like a mini-SUV, the Vibe shares the other characteristics of the Matrix. But the Vibe shares much more than just the target market and sales points of the Matrix: Toyota manufactures the drive train for the Vibe; in fact, it's the same power plant and transmission as for the Matrix.

In the Vibe and Matrix, we have the classic teaming-up strategy. Toyota wants to fully utilize its manufacturing operation and it's quite willing to sell engines and transmissions to GM. So, Toyota wins whether it sells a Matrix or GM sells a Vibe. GM on the other hand, needs reliable, efficient, competitively priced components in order to be successful in the small car market, a market that GM de-emphasized years before. Indeed, most consumers see the Toyota components as a plus in their car-buying review. By delivering a quality product to younger buyers, GM and its Pontiac brand are also creating the foundation for brand

> ### First Thought Is to the Endgame
>
> Corporate alliances, joint ventures, and teaming-up strate-
> gies can be very effective ways to deliver more by owning
> less of the value chain and thus increasing returns on investment.
> However, smart companies structure these alliances very carefully, with
> particular emphasis on the end. Our first thought in considering a team-
> ing-up strategy should be on how we get out of the relationship, even if
> the results are good.
>
> Sometimes working together can be too stressful for both parties,
> whatever the market success, so the deal must be severed. For exam-
> ple, if risk tolerances of the two organizations differ widely, it's difficult
> to continue to work together.
>
> Therefore, these contingencies must be confronted in advance of
> the deal. Among the issues to be addressed: How much lead time is
> necessary? Who gets which assets? What about ongoing customer
> service? What will a divorce cost each party?

loyalty that's so important in determining the future car-buying practices of consumers.

Consider the Walgreens value migration strategy. The basic idea is to use the convenience and traffic associated with the drug store and deliver more and different value opportunities for the consumer. Walgreens is building more and more stand-alone stores to support this approach and deliver growth.

Using the grocery platform as a source for value migration is becoming very popular. Most new grocery stores include a bank, a café, a drug store, a floral shop, and a liquor and wine store. Some of these are in-house efforts, some occur through acquisitions, while others are teaming-up strategies with brand-ed partners.

A good example of using the grocery platform is Albertsons, based in Boise. In the 1960s, Albertsons teamed up with Skaggs drug stores to provide an in-store pharmacy and over-the-count-er drug and related items. This partnership ended in 1977. Over time Skagg became American Stores Company and acquired Jewel Companies, a Chicago-based food store that owned Osco Drug Stores and Lucky Stores, a California-based grocer. In

1999, Albertsons acquired American Stores, completing the circle that began with Skaggs. Now Albertsons and Jewel stores each co-brand stores with Osco Drug, highlighting the strong brands of each firm.

In evaluating whether a teaming-up strategy makes sense for us, the first consideration is likely to be identifying areas where we lack expertise, scale, or brand presence in a current market situation. At the same time, if our business could benefit by renewed focus on our core components, then finding a good partner will free our management to recommit to our customers. In order to be successful, though, we must consider all the possible futures: What will customers think and do? What will competitors do? What if the market changes? What if this doesn't work? What happens if our partnership is wildly successful? Smart managers imagine these future scenarios before entering a teaming-up arrangement for three reasons:

- to determine whether it makes sense to team up
- to find the best partner
- to outline the structure of such a deal

Digital Delivery

The Internet and the digitization of communications (cell phones) have been the innovations with the most impact on the daily lives of most people around the world over the last 10 years. Of course, these innovations have created tremendous business opportunities in all areas of commerce. This is the digital delivery strategy, to use the innovation of Internet and digital technology to create a new business model for existing and new products and services.

Two of the more powerful examples of digital delivery, both demonstrating new business models, are eBay and Napster. Both of these examples used the power of Internet-based technology in new ways to offer large numbers of consumers an innovative approach to either buying and selling virtually anything (eBay) and acquiring music (Napster).

eBay is a site at which one can sell or buy virtually anything. The best way to understand eBay is to go to the site (www.ebay.com) and look around. Shop, but pay attention to the rules of the auction. Look for the tips for buying and bidding strategy. Notice the ratings systems that help potential buyers feel more confident

> ### The Net Is Not Magic
>
> The success of some companies in using the Internet should not lead you to believe that it's magic. A recent news story suggested that in the three years, 2000-2003, some 4,800 Internet companies have vanished—either acquired or shut down. So, treat it as a means for your strategies, not as magic.

using the site. Scan the vast array of products and services that are available, featured, and promoted on the site. Check out the partnerships that have been forged with eBay for the resale of a variety of goods, used cars in particular.

> ### Be Prepared for the Future
>
> In 1991, Alvin Toffler followed up his successful book *Future Shock,* with a futurist book called *The Third Wave.* The principal idea of the book is that humanity has known two "waves" of progress: we moved from hunting and gathering to agriculture and then we changed our economic base from agricultural to industrial. Toffler argued that now we're engaged in the third wave. One of the major insights he offered is what he called the rise of *prosumers*—individuals and organizations that simultaneously were producers and consumers of goods or services. Toffler's examples showed that businesses could off-load costs of production to consumers by having them assume some of the responsibilities and functions of production. When we pump our own gas or bag our own groceries, for example, we're assuming a role in the delivery of the goods we're buying.
>
> The Internet makes prosuming that much easier. Companies can off-load work to their customers, whether in making travel plans or Web-based (self-service) customer support. Astute companies can see the future better by reading about and testing alternatives proposed by futurists like Toffler. By getting ahead of the others, companies can find market and financial advantages.

eBay may be the strongest Internet company ever. Replacing classifieds, garage sales, and estate auctions via technology, thereby giving sellers a worldwide marketplace for their goods, eBay has initiated a whole new way for buyers and sellers to connect, bargain, and transact.

Napster is similar in its technology-based, revolutionary impact, but has experienced a very different outcome. Napster was a technology that permitted file sharing among vast numbers of individuals linked through the Internet. Napster was created in 1999 to allow subscribers to exchange music (MP3 and other file formats). Users would download free Napster software, search other users' music files for the selections of interest, and then copy the files located. In essence, Napster was the electronic equivalent of borrowing a music tape from a neighbor and making a copy.

As the popularity and ease of Napster became apparent to the music industry, however, the issues became more significant. Artists were not being compensated for their work, copyright protections were being ignored and abused, and the music industry was losing business. Some performers and companies took legal action and Napster was closed down. That's not the end of the story, though, as Napster clones have sprung up and the reality of the ubiquitous digital delivery of music is clear. Few have little doubt that music will be delivered to consumers in different ways than today, as different as vinyl records are from CDs.

A digital delivery strategy requires completely understanding the customers' needs and uses of product and services and using that information to work with technology experts to deliver something that creates real value for the buyer and real returns for the investors. AOL, Amazon, CNET, Orbitz, and others have shown staying power in their fields; many other areas are still emerging.

Deep Connections

The deep connections strategy, while very successful for those companies employing it, cannot just be implemented like all of these other ideas. In some sense, deep connections must be earned over time. The strategy means that we appeal to the emotional components of buyers' psyches, in addition to their functional or financial considerations.

The best example of deep connections is Harley-Davidson Motorcycles. Harley has created a bond with its customers in a way few other companies can replicate. Harley owners gather through the company-facilitated Harley Owners Groups (commonly known as HOGs). In addition to all sorts of motorcycle accessories, such as most companies might offer to customers, Harley has been extraordinarily successful at marketing clothes and other branded merchandise to its loyal customers. Indeed, as mentioned in Chapter 4, Ford has begun to market a Harley-Davidson truck—using the brand (as it did with Eddie Bauer) to reach Harley owners looking for a four-wheeled ride. By creating this attachment with the brand, Harley virtually ensures loyalty in parts and replacement bike sales.

It can be argued that others have created a deep connections approach like Harley, Coca-Cola, and the Oprah Winfrey complex of businesses, for example. While a company can plan to use this tactic as a method of survival and sustenance, it's an approach that requires cultivation. Buick, in its current ad campaign, using the persona of historic GM designer Harley Earl and throwback cosmetics (the three "Ventiports" on the front quarter panel of the Park Avenue, a Buick trademark introduced in 1949), is looking to capitalize on nostalgia with a growing aging population, its traditional market. Deep connections are not something that you can try for a while, then drop, then try again: you either have them or not. The jury is still out on Buick.

ASAP

Speed is the key—do it faster means do it better. In many markets this is true. One-hour dry cleaning, fast food, quick oil changes, drive-through service, over-the-counter pregnancy tests, and instant messaging are but a few of the examples of our life in the fast lane. Consumers often look for convenience,

Time Is on Our Side

Smart Managing   While speed can be a very important component of our strategy in some instances, in others we might want to look to the slower pace of yesteryear. Starbucks delivers your coffee made-to-order and quickly; you can often even use a drive-up window. But Starbucks provides a place for leisure for others, a calm, comfortable setting for conversation, a crossword, or just contemplation—along with their java. By using time as a strategy, fast for some and slow for others, Starbucks broadens its appeal and grows.

as defined by speed, in the products and services they need. This is the ASAP strategy. To use this approach, we need to understand whether we're delivering more value to customers by delivering sooner.

Federal Express is the poster child for the ASAP strategy. FedEx created a new business model, a new operational model, and a relief to procrastinators all over the world. FedEx saw the unmet need for immediate, next-day guaranteed delivery. Whether packages or letters, FedEx relied on the last-minute urgency required in business. FedEx also played against the U.S. Postal Service's poor delivery reputation to build a market position. The message, "When it absolutely, positively has to be there overnight," told consumers everything they needed to know about FedEx. The price may be high, but the goods will get there overnight.

In today's markets, the overnight delivery service is a mature business. Now. virtually every delivery service competitor offers the same services as FedEx, including the U.S. Postal Service. Growth has been boosted by the expansion of catalog and Internet purchases that require delivery services and an assimilation of the overnight phenomenon as a regular part of our business culture. There's no doubt that the emergence of FedEx and its speed strategy changed the way business was done in the U.S. and all over the world.

Customization

When we see an opportunity to create value for customers by allowing them to design products specifically for their needs or circumstances, that's a customization strategy. By creating the perception and/or reality of this customized, unique product or service delivery, we engender a strong affinity with buyers, leading to higher price points and greater loyalty than with mass-produced goods.

An excellent example of this approach is a market-leading company in the golf business, Karsten Manufacturing. Karsten Solheim made an impact in the golf business first with his design of putters. Using an original heel-toe weighting design, the engineer, Solheim, eliminated much of the twisting associated with off-center hits. Because his first putter made a distinctive sound when striking the ball, his clubs were labeled Ping. In the early 1970s, Solheim entered the market for irons. One innovation he used to gain product and market advantage was to customize the sets of irons to the buyer. With a simple color code and a few measurements from customers, Ping irons were adjusted in the lie (angle to the turf), grip size (size of hand), and shaft length. As a result, Ping clubs were the first in the market to use investment casting as the manufacturing advantage and the first to be customized to each golfer as a marketing (and performance) advantage. The results have been spectacular. Even today Ping promotes its custom fitting and custom building of clubs as a differentiator in the marketplace.

As another example of customization, look at your homepage. Yahoo! wants to be the homepage of choice for all Internet users, with My Yahoo!. One method for appealing to such a broad market is to let each individual customize his or her content, colors, and layout. The ability to track selected stocks, sports results, and weather locations creates a strong bond between the user and the homepage provider. While Yahoo! may have initiated the customization capability, now all homepage vendors offer the same service.

To employ a customization strategy, we must explore whether customers will perceive added value because of the custom features. To return to an example cited earlier, Dell builds computers to customer specs and has become the leading computer seller. Of course, if we choose this approach, we must deliver real custom differentiation, so that the products or services are personalized to the buyer or at least the buyer perceives them to be so.

A key factor in determining whether this strategy can work is the time needed for custom work, compared with the buyer's tolerance for waiting. Cars can be made to order, but most people will compromise because when they see a car they like, they want an immediate delivery. Most cars are built based on past experiences and stocked for sale. Custom orders are a small part of the business.

Mass Market

The evolution of many products or product features is from niche markets to broad markets. Companies that have been successful at mass-marketing strategies—extending a product to the mass market—have been very well rewarded.

> **Key Term**
>
> **Mass market** To offer and sell goods or services to the broad population, not just market segments. Mass marketing presents the products to all demographic (income, gender, age) and geographic segments. With a mass-market approach, anyone is a potential buyer.

Think back to when only a few could afford a car phone. At first, a car phone was the size of a regular home phone and its electronics package in the trunk was also substantial. Companies like Motorola and Qualcomm (among others) really worked at slimming down the electronics. Soon the notion of a car phone vanished, replaced by the cell phone used anywhere and everywhere. It's hard to imagine now that only a few years ago, cell phones (originally bag phones) were the exception, not the rule.

Wal-Mart grew to be the biggest retailer, in part, by bringing the discount department store to rural America, the only geographic region not served by mass merchandisers. In its wake, many small businesses have failed, but in return rural areas got access to broad product inventories at very low prices. Of course, Wal-Mart's strategy did not end with rural markets, but continued into suburban markets, and now into urban markets. In these later phases, the Wal-Mart approach is clear: low prices.

Fix-It-for-Me

The strategy of fix-it-for-me takes the following perspective: identify a customer problem, identify a comprehensive solution, and package the solution in a single product, as a complete solution. The appeal of this approach to the customer is obvious: if I purchase the product, I have everything I need to solve my problem. The difficulty for the producer is that finding a comprehensive solution may require going beyond the walls of the existing business, which means finding partners or expertise in new areas.

TurboTax is a piece of software for the personal computer. In the package the software provides everything that a taxpayer needs to complete the annual tax ritual, including all of the forms, calculations, and the capability for electronic filing. The program has become very easy to use, even providing tips and signaling potential missed deductions along the way. Most importantly, annual changes in the tax law are built into the program, so that TurboTax really does solve the taxpayer's problem, with a single solution that allows accurate and effective filing of federal and state income tax forms. It may not have been the first tax software package, but it's now the top-selling tax software program in the United States.

Another example of the fix-it-for-me approach is Nicoderm CQ, the over-the-counter smoking cessation program. A smoker who's committed to quitting smoking can purchase this product and get everything, including quasi-psychological advice, in order to stop the smoking habit. The product includes a three-step process for reducing the effects of nicotine withdrawal over time, so that a smoker can ease out of the smoking routine.

Fix-it-for-me, more than other strategies, highlights the need to put ourselves in the shoes of our customers to discover their unmet needs. However, it's critically important with any strategy that companies truly understand their target customers' needs and behaviors. There's no substitute for high-quality market research, via surveys, focus groups, or interviews.

Fix-it-for-me also reminds us that we may need to think beyond our company in order to deliver a comprehensive solution. Customers may want services or features that we're unable to deliver without the aid of other organizations. The key to success with fix-it-for-me strategies is that the product package solves the customer's total problem. We can't really leave pieces outside the package if we want to get the full benefit of the strategy.

This Is Interesting, but What Do I Do Now?

We have presented 10 of the best business strategies in history and given examples of how various businesses have used the strategies. Possibly one or more of these strategies can be successful for our firm in our markets. How do we know?

The answer comes from the people in the company. Here's an approach that can work to test whether it's worthwhile trying to steal any of these ideas. Pull together a cross-functional and diverse team of individuals. The group should include accountants, marketers, production people, customer service staff, and others. The levels can vary, but I suggest that the group be made up of managers and above; managers understand the functions well but also typically have experience in the business and are used to communicating across levels. You can have more than one group, so limit each to seven people. School the groups on the Top 10 strategies, with either a presentation or this text.

Assign each group the following task:

What are the three best ideas for our company that borrow one of these 10 concepts? Be prepared to give a presentation explaining the power of each idea for our company to senior staff.

Give each group a hard deadline, like four to six hours. At the end of the time, assemble all the groups and let the presentations begin. If past success is a guide, you will get two or three really good ideas for your business, ready to be researched and developed.

Manager's Checklist for Chapter 9

❏ We can innovate by imitating successful strategies of other firms and adopting them for your company.

❏ For each of the ten tried and true, successful strategies detailed in this chapter, the company must understand unmet customer needs completely.

❏ Use a diverse group to choose which approaches can work in your company. Be sure to give a firm, tight deadline and an important task, like presentation to a supportive senior staff. Follow up on the best ideas.

Implementing Strategic Decisions

W e've defined business strategy and discussed strategy
development in terms of ideas, purpose, advantage, customers, product, market, and ways of doing business.

We've covered vision, mission, and goals. We've evaluated
performance and studied our situation, with four types of analysis—environmental (social factors, economic factors, political
and regulatory factors, and technological factors), industry
(structure, evolution, and competition), internal (structure,
resources, and culture), and SWOT (strengths, weaknesses,
opportunities, and threats).

We've outlined strategic choices—generic strategies, positioning, and execution—and considered seven classes of strategies. We've discussed strategic thinking, in terms of optimizing
our assets (tangible and intangible), analyzing our core business, working that core, and making the most of adjacencies.
We've followed up with the strategic thinking involved in 10
strategies.

Now what?

This chapter is all about executing the chosen strategy—organizing the company, making the necessary adjustments, and measuring the results—in order to reach the stated goals.

Strategic Decision Making

One method to showcase the best way to accomplish something is to highlight the reasons why others fail. A recent article in *Sloan Management Review*[1] detailed the principal causes of strategy failures. In short, the article finds that top management's attitudes, communication, and commitment (or lack thereof) to the plan were the leading contributors to failure. Here are the specific causes found by the research:

- top-down or laissez-faire senior management style
- unclear strategy and conflicting priorities
- ineffective senior management team
- poor vertical communication
- poor coordination across functions, businesses, or borders
- inadequate down-the-line leadership skills and development

If we study this list and look at the research, we can come to a few conclusions about the correct way to implement strategy to avoid the pitfalls cited by the article. We believe that there are four principles to adopt from these research findings.

Four Key Principles

First, senior managers need to see the role of the entire organization in fulfilling the strategy. They must engage all levels of the organization. It's not enough for the senior management team to go to an off-site retreat and then come back to the organization with strategy pronouncements. Successful companies realize that strategic insights can be found everywhere in the company and by anyone. In addition to finding ideas throughout the company, companies that use broad and deep

[1] Michael Beer and Russell A. Eisenstat, "The Silent Killers of Strategy Implementation and Learning," *MIT Sloan Management Review,* Summer 2000, pp. 29-40.

Strategic Thinking at DEMCO

Bill Stroner, CEO of DEMCO, Inc., a direct marketer of supplies and equipment to libraries, wanted to energize the company to find growth initiatives. The goals of the company were clear, but the opportunities in the library business seemed limited. Stroner believed that business ideas, both long and short term, were not in short supply at DEMCO; in fact, every manager could contribute to the positioning of the company.

As a result, Stroner pulled the entire management staff away from the company for two days to find the company's direction. They identified five initiatives and Stroner organized multifunctional task forces to move from ideas to actions. Within a year, the company had implemented most of the actions and had closed on a significant acquisition, which was one of the key initiatives. The trust placed in the employees paid tremendous dividends in the ability of the firm to seize the momentum captured by the retreat and act on the initiatives.

organizational involvement will find that strategy implementation, which takes place at all levels, will be easier. Employees will be more enthusiastic and less cynical about the strategic initiatives if they have been involved in developing them and designing the alignment of the organizational components.

The second principle based upon these findings is that the vision, goals, and strategy need to be clear and clearly communicated throughout the company and that decisions need to be consistent with these ideals. Companies need to work at communicating the business strategy to ensure that the entire organization is on the same page. And this is another reason why broad involvement at all levels is important. If line managers are informed and enthusiastic, they can be the best resource for strengthening the communication of the message throughout the company. However, nothing can destroy a message quicker than decisions that appear to be in conflict with the strategic direction of the company. When executives make such a decision, they must support it with good communication regarding why they made it and how it's consistent with the business strategy. If they cannot explain their decision, maybe they should rethink it.

The third principle is that senior managers must align the strategy with the execution capabilities of the business (resources, operations, and organization). All substructures of the organization must be motivated to act in the best interests of the total company. One of the reasons that Demco's initiatives were adopted and

> ### Is It Consistent with Our Strategy?
>
> That's the question that senior managers should ask about every decision they consider. It may seem obvious, but many decisions don't face that challenge. This is especially true in areas of information technology. Many decisions to invest in technology seem to be based more on what's available than on what's appropriate for the strategy of the organization.

implemented so quickly and so well is that the CEO immediately formed multifunctional teams to lead the effort for each idea. By doing so, he got alignment among and between the various units and created an environment in which turf battles were minimized.

Finally, leaders at all levels need to have the skills and tools to drive the strategy through all activities of the organization. The real action in a business takes place where the transactions occur. The customer sales and service interactions, negotiating with suppliers, and producing and filling orders are the heart and soul of any business. In each of these areas, down-the-line leaders and managers need to be prepared and equipped

> ### Gap Analysis
>
> To make sure that leaders at all levels have the skills and knowledge to drive the strategy, conduct a gap analysis. Start with four simple questions:
> - What is your strategy?
> - What capabilities do your leaders need to execute this strategy?
> - Which of these capabilities do they possess?
> - How can they acquire the capabilities that they lack?
>
> Gap analysis can help you make sure that your people have the skills to implement the strategy and that you don't waste money and time on unproductive approaches to training.

to deal with implementing the strategic direction. Trust and empowerment free employees to do business; skills and tools give them the best shot at doing it well. Companies need to assess which particular tools and skills are important for their strategy and ensure that these capabilities exist in the key areas.

A System for Implementing Strategy: The Balanced Scorecard

Let's review! We began with vision and goals, clearly articulated. Next we examined the current position of the firm relative to those goals and the markets. We compiled intensive, comprehensive data on our customers and non-customers to identify their unmet needs and buying behaviors. We looked at the external environment to trace trends and competitor activity. Finally, we looked at our internal capabilities and created an inventory of our strengths, weaknesses, opportunities, and threats.

Using this information, resources throughout the organization, and the methods outlined in the strategic thinking chapters, we identified potential strategies to pursue our vision and achieve our goals. After testing these potential initiatives against our execution capabilities, we chose a path for action. We then laid out the strategy with positioning aligned with resources, operations, and the organization. Now it's time to implement the strategy. So, how do we do it?

The best answer is to establish a system that communicates regularly on progress toward our goals to all levels of the organization. This system needs to capture what's important to our vision and monitor progress on goal metrics, but also on our pursuit of the vision. This system is called *the balanced scorecard*.

The balanced scorecard is a systematic approach for creating what the authors, Robert. S. Kaplan and David P. Norton, call the strategy-focused organization.[2] The balanced scorecard is a method for mapping the anticipated effects of strategy and

[2] Robert S. Kaplan and David P. Norton, *The Strategy-Focused Organization* (Boston: Harvard Business School Press, 2000).

measuring the right items to inform the business about whether the strategy is succeeding or not.

Elements of the Balanced Scorecard Approach

The balanced scorecard begins with a simple but critical notion, that our vision and goals affect three constituencies: the shareholders, the customers, and the employees. Consequently, we

Balanced scorecard An approach to strategic management proposed by Robert S. Kaplan and David P. Norton in "Balanced Scorecard: Measures That Drive Performance," (*Harvard Business Review*, January-February, 1992). The balanced scorecard provides a framework for considering strategy from four perspectives: financial, customer, business processes, and learning and growth. Kaplan and Norton developed the balanced scorecard because of the limitations of managing only by financial measures.

should map and measure the effects of our strategy on each of these groups. There's a fourth dimension to the balanced scorecard, though—our internal business processes. In each case, the way we influence and improve the company is through what we do and how we do it. Therefore, the balanced scorecard looks at effects of the strategic initiatives on those business processes. Kaplan and Norton divided their balanced scorecard into four areas:

- financial
- customer
- internal
- learning and growth

In each of these areas, the company identifies four items:

- objectives
- measures
- targets
- initiatives, based upon the vision, goals, and chosen strategy

By creating a strategy map, linking the elements of the strategy to each area and the related components, the balanced

scorecard and the strategy are woven throughout the organization. (For more detailed information about the balanced scorecard, visit the Balanced Scorecard Collaborative Web site,
www.bscol.com.)

Balanced Scorecard in Action

The best way to understand how the balanced scorecard works
is to see it in action. Let's apply the balanced scorecard to that
Italian restaurant business idea that we introduced in Chapter 1.
We're going to help the owner install a balanced scorecard system to drive the business, through the strategy, to his vision. By
this example, you'll see how the pieces fit together and the
business operates to achieve its goals. We won't be able to
show every aspect of strategy implementation using the balanced scorecard, but this example will show how strategy
comes alive using the approach.

Background

Ben has a vision of a great business. His restaurant, to be called
La Casa di Poggi (named after his grandfather), will ultimately
be recognized as the best Italian restaurant in the region.
Patrons will love the place for its food and ambiance. The
employees will be able to earn a good living and have solid
benefits. The restaurant should earn a target 20% return on
investment. Ben can see the concept expanding to other locations and, in the longer term, going public. His vision is so clear
that he can actually see himself greeting guests delighted to be
having dinner at La Casa di Poggi and saying goodbye as they
leave, fully satisfied and gladly paying their bill and leaving generous tips for the wait staff. He sees his guests as adults out for
an excellent dinner at their favorite place. He imagines that they
will have a good time, see some friends, and return often.

For the sake of simplicity here, we'll assume that Ben has
secured a location, made improvements, installed the equipment, and hired the employees. (Of course, the decisions
involved in these actions would necessarily involve strategic
thinking.) He knows what he wants, but now he must craft a

strategy to get there.

Strategy

Ben wants high returns for his investment. To get them, he knows that the restaurant must be filled, every table, every night, from open to close. His pride and his business thinking tell him that the strategy that will achieve that goal includes two components: outstanding food quality, presentation, and taste, and an experience that creates a demand. Ben believes that if he can deliver on these two dimensions, La Casa di Poggi will be full.

However, being full does not guarantee those 20% returns. Ben realizes that he needs an operating strategy throughout the restaurant that delivers the profit levels that he desires. The costs of the ingredients for the meals are probably not a place where savings can be found. First, the goal of outstanding food requires top-of-the-line, higher-cost ingredients. Second, with a single start-up location, La Casa di Poggi will not generate enough volume to qualify for deep discounts from suppliers. Therefore, if Ben wants to achieve high margins, the solution must lie in menu selection and pricing. Ben's strategy is to offer moderate pricing, consistent with the goal of encouraging patrons to return often. So, to hit his profit target, Ben makes the following three strategic food decisions:

1. very selective choices of food items
2. smaller portions
3. à la carte menu

The menu offerings will be chosen with extreme care; in fact, Ben believes this is the key to making the business work to meet his goals. The objective is to find authentic Italian items, prepare them exquisitely, but make choices that include low-cost ingredients. The idea is to offer excellent dining, at moderate prices, but with dishes made from rather ordinary items. There will be no abalone or lobster items, for example. When pricier items, like veal, are used, smaller portions will keep the price/cost ratio in balance and in line with the target margins. Finally, by employing an à la carte approach, in which every item is priced moderately, but separately, the restaurant will allow the patrons to determine the level of their bills.

In addition, Ben decides to serve quality wines and liquors, but will use a very high mark-up strategy on drink items. Ben believes, based on some focus group work, that when people recommend a restaurant, they do so based on the food and its pricing and the wine selection, but not the wine pricing. The beverage line will be a heavy profit contributor.

Finally, Ben wants to be a good employer, providing good pay and benefits. He also knows loyal employees provide better customer service. In this matter, the strategies for customers and employees are very well aligned. Ben's approach is for base pay and benefits to be moderate, but for the à la carte menu and the wine list to present opportunities for the wait staff to bulk up the bill and receive bigger tips. Ben will put in place a cash profit-sharing plan to reward all employees, as an incentive to achieve profit targets.

Balanced Scorecard: La Casa di Poggi

Knowing the strategy, we can now employ the balanced scorecard system of mapping the strategy onto an implementation design. For each of the four areas—financial, customer, process, and employee—we will create a program of communication and monitoring that includes goals, measures, targets, and initiatives. With this structure, we can align the various pieces and ensure that we make progress toward the vision. Figure 10-1 depicts an abbreviated scorecard for the restaurant. The strategy map shows the linkages between the elements; next to each area is the measure the company will use to monitor progress.

Financial Perspective. Like most businesses, La Casa di Poggi seeks return on investment and growth. Profitability is key for two reasons. First, Ben's business idea and investment should be rewarded. Second, any future plan to raise capital for expansion will depend upon showing investors a superior ROI. For these reasons, we'll use ROI as our measure of profitability. We might use return on sales, but it does not convey the same discipline

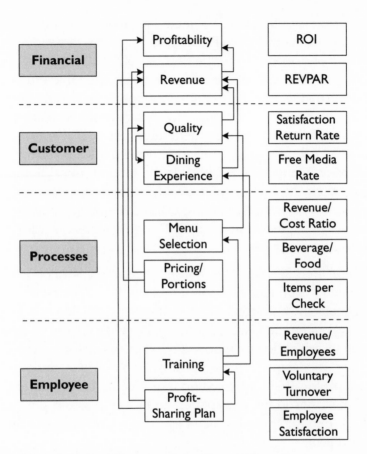

Figure 10-1. Balanced scorecard, La Casa di Poggi

as ROI with respect to the total capital used by the business. Notice that the strategy map links profitability to revenue, but also directly to the pricing/portions approach that Ben is taking.

As a start-up, La Casa di Poggi must attract patrons. Revenue in the strategy is based upon the quality and dining experience of the customers, but is also directly related to the à la carte strategy and the profit-sharing plan instituted for employees. Our expectation is that, through the profit-sharing incentives, all employees will promote the quality and dining experience of the operation. Furthermore, the wait staff will more actively see themselves as sales and service providers.

The measure that we've selected for revenue is revenue per available reservation (REVPAR). Each evening, depending upon the hours of operation and the number of tables, we offer a specific number of reservations. For example, one table may be sold or turned two or three times. Suppose that on any given evening we have a maximum of 50 reservations available, REVPAR monitors the dollars generated per available table. Thus REVPAR, in a single measure, monitors sales relative to capacity or occupancy. REVPAR is the kind of measure that can be posted on the wall daily or weekly, to communicate to the entire staff how effectively we're using the space. Once the tables are filled, increasing REVPAR requires greater sales per table or higher prices.

Customer Perspective. The marketing strategy is to offer a great dining experience for the target market. If we achieve that goal consistently, patrons will be extremely satisfied and they will return often. La Casa di Poggi will rely on a word-of-mouth campaign, which keeps marketing expenses low and creates strong relationships with the patrons. Ben believes, and he can cite examples, that by exploiting free media, like restaurant reviews, stories in the newspaper, and local business publications, he can minimize the need for paid advertising and thus increase profits.

For customer measures, then, satisfaction is critical. Ben should set very high targets for customer satisfaction, since this is a key metric for the success of the strategy. He decides on a satisfaction initiative that includes the following components:

- Set quality, dining experience, and intent to return or recommend to others as separate measures to be monitored through customer surveys.
- Purchase a handheld system for recording these satisfaction surveys at tableside. This ensures that every reservation is polled and the results can be linked to wait staff, day of week, and entrée selection. The system can also be used to document the number of returning customers.

Internal Business Processes. The key internal business processes for La Casa di Poggi relate to ensuring quality and generating revenue and profit. Ben's strategy is to create menu options have high appeal for customers, but also have high margins. Metrics to monitor these factors include the following three:

- Revenue/Cost ratio: On a weekly basis, score the food revenue generated by the cost of the food inputs acquired during the week. This measurement accounts for both the cost of food and the level of waste. Also, as pricing of food items changes, this metric will help to manage prices for the customers.
- Beverage/Food ratio: We know that wine and bar items are a great source of revenue and profit. Tracking the ratio of beverage revenues to food revenues tells how effective the wait staff is at selling the beverage line and provides information about segments of our clientele. For example, if the ratio is going down, we may wish to promote the restaurant more directly to consumers with an appreciation of wine.
- Items per check: The à la carte menu strategy is intended to generate revenue by pricing items individually. By monitoring the items sold on each check, we can adjust pricing and sales techniques to increase revenues.

Employee Perspective. The issues that revolve around employees are the final piece of La Casa di Poggi's balanced scorecard. Training is an important part of the strategy. All employees need to be trained in the important strategic dimensions of quality, a great dining experience, and Italian cooking and wine. Wait staff in particular need sales training and education on how to rescue an endangered customer experience. Ben believes in a staff that's empowered and trained. The other dimension of the employee strategy is the profit-sharing plan. This plan aims at achieving two objectives. First, employees have some "skin in the game," a personal investment in providing a great customer experience. Second, the incentive relates directly to profitability and all the drivers designed in the strategy: La Casa di

Balanced Scorecard Works for All

The balanced scorecard helps managers translate mission and strategy into specific objectives and measures. It can be used in any organization. What will work for Ben and La Casa di Poggi has worked for huge corporations, such as Mobil Oil. In the words of R.J. McCool, Executive Vice President of Mobil, "The balanced scorecard has served as an irreplaceable agenda for discussion of business strategies, strengths, weaknesses, and performance."

Poggi will pay extra cash to employees when it can afford to, not as a fixed cost.

To monitor the employee issues, the following metrics are recommended:

- **Revenue per Employee:** Headcount is one of the most important categories of expense. Increasing revenue per employee may mean greater productivity. It also measures how effectively the business is selling.
- **Voluntary Turnover:** The quality and dining experience of the patrons depend on the service levels and competence of the staff; if turnover is high, service and customer satisfaction will suffer. Also, since training is important and expensive, the company cannot afford to lose people regularly.
- **Employee Satisfaction:** This is important for two reasons. First, it lets us know whether the business model is working for the employees' benefit. Second, only satisfied employees can deliver service that satisfies the customer, so we want to do things that keep employees satisfied.

Balanced Scorecard: Summary

No single example can fully explore the robustness of the balanced scorecard method for implementing strategy. This very simple case is intended to show how strategic thinking can be translated into an executable plan. Furthermore, a key idea is to construct measures, targets, and initiatives so that management can assess progress and adjust activities.

The balanced scorecard can be applied to any type of organization. Its structures and linkages provide the framework for implementing strategies and judging the results.

Change

Few things work perfectly. It's unlikely that any strategy will achieve the desired results without some changes. Strategy needs to be continuously developed and iteratively improved. We cannot expect that an annual strategic planning session will answer our business questions until the same time next year. That's why metrics are so important. The things we measure should tell us whether our assumptions are valid and show us trends. Measures will also tell us about our competitors and what our customers are thinking and doing. Measurements tell us how we're doing in terms of benchmarks and targets. It's both normal and necessary to use these tools to make adjustments in our approaches. So when changes are indicated, go back to the starting point of this book and begin again.

A Final Thought

This book is all about building successful strategies. The process involves three steps:

- knowing
- thinking
- doing

Knowing means ...

... that we understand our goals and objectives.

... that we understand our company, our markets, our target customers, and the relevant environments that affect the future of our business.

Thinking means ...

... that we use the information to plan and plot the path to success.

... that we get every member of the entire organization involved in a process to design the way to reach our goals.

... that we soberly assess our strengths, weaknesses, opportunities, and threats.

... that we test strategic ideas against the realities of our capabilities, and the reaction of customers and competitors.

Doing means ...

... that we make decisions.

... that we communicate clearly and often.

... that we strive for results and measure those results against the standards established by our vision.

... that we continually reassess our strategy and refine both the process and the actions necessary to meet our goals.

When you mention "business strategy," many people think of a fog, some buzzwords, and cool charts from consultants and MBAs. This book's intent was to make strategy real, exciting, and within reach of every manager. Enlightened companies realize that good strategic business ideas come from every corner of the organization. By providing a toolkit for knowing and thinking and doing strategy, we hope that this book helps you and your organization reach your vision and goals with certainty. Good luck!

Manager's Checklist for Chapter 10

❑ The principal causes of strategy failures are the attitudes, communication, and commitment of senior managers, specifically the following:
- top-down or laissez-faire senior management style
- unclear strategy and conflicting priorities
- ineffective senior management team

- • poor vertical communication
- • poor coordination across functions, businesses, or borders
- • inadequate down-the-line leadership skills and development

❏ Senior managers need to see the role of the entire organization in fulfilling the strategy. They must engage all levels of the organization.

❏ Senior managers must make the vision, goals, and strategy clear, they must effectively communicate them throughout the company, and their decisions need to be consistent with these ideals.

❏ Senior managers must align the strategy with the execution capabilities of the business (resources, operations, and organization). All substructures of the organization must be motivated to act in the best interests of the total company.

❏ Leaders at all levels need to have the skills and tools to drive the strategy through all activities of the organization. Down-the-line managers need to be prepared to deal with implementing the strategic direction.

❏ The best system for implementing strategies is the balanced scorecard, a systematic approach for creating the strategy-focused organization.

❏ Building a successful strategies process involves three steps:
- • knowing
- • thinking
- • doing

References for Strategic Planning

The following is a list pf books I have found useful in thinking about and implementing strategy. They include references I used in developing this book.

David A. Aaker, *Developing Business Strategies* (New York: John Wiley & Sons, 2001).

Patrick J. Below, George L. Morrisey, and Betty L. Acomb, *The Executive Guide to Strategic Planning* (San Francisco: Josey-Bass, 1987).

Richard E. S. Boulton, Barry D. Libert, and Steve M. Samek, *Cracking the Value Code: How Successful Buisnesses are Creating Wealth in the New Economy* (New York: HarperCollins, Publishers, 2000).

Brent Bowers and Deidre Leipziger, *The New York Times Management Reader* (New York: Henry Holt and Company, 2001).

Frank Caropreso, *Getting Value from Strategic Planning* (New York: The Conference Board, 1988).

Jim Collins, *Good to Great: Why Some Companies Make the Leap ... and Others Don't* (New York: HarperCollins, Publishers, 2001).

George S. Day, *Market Driven Strategy: Processes for Creating Value* (New York: The Free Press, 1999).

Cornelis A. De Kluyver, *Strategic Thinking: An Executive Perspective* (Upper Saddle River, NJ: Prentice Hall, 2000).

Larry Downes, *The Strategy Machine: Building Your Business One Idea at a Time* (New York: HarperBusiness, 2002).

Peter F. Drucker, *The Essential Drucker* (New York: HarperCollins, Publishers, 2001).

Evan M. Dudik, *Strategic Renaissance: New Thinking and Innovate Tools to Create Great Corporate Strategies* (New York: AMACOM, 2000).

C. Davis Fogg, *Team-Based Strategic Planning: A Complete Guide to Structuring, Facilitating, and Implementing the Process* (New York: AMACOM, 1994).

James L. Heskett, W. Earl Sasser, Jr., and Leonard A. Schlesinger, *The Service Profit Chain* (New York: The Free Press, 1997).

Frances Hesselbein and Rob Johnston, *On High-Performance Organizations* (San Francisco: Jossey-Bass, 2002).

Per Jenster and David Hussey, *Company Analysis: Determining Strategic Capability* (West Sussex, England: John Wiley & Sons, Ltd., 2001).

Arnold S. Judson, *Making Strategy Happen: Transforming Plans into Reality* (Cambridge, MA: Basil Blackwell, Inc., 1990).

Robert S. Kaplan and David P. Norton, *The Strategy-Focused Organization* (Boston: Harvard Business School Press, 2001).

Tom Kelley with Jonathan Littman, *The Art of Innovation: Lessons in Creativity from IDEO, America's Leading Design Firm* (New York: Doubleday, 2001).

Richard A. Luecke, *Scuttle Your Ships Before Advancing and Other Lessons from History on Leadership and Change for Today's Managers* (New York: Oxford University Press, 1994).

John D. Martin and J. William Petty, *Value-Based Management: The Corporate Response to the Shareholder Revolution* (Boston: Harvard Business School Press, 2000).

Shiv S. Mathur and Alfred Kenyon, *Creating Value: Successful Business Strategies* (Woburn, MA: Butterworth-Heinemann, 2001).

Patrick Thurbin, *Playing the Strategy Game* (London: Pearson Education, 2001).

Chris Zook with James Allen, *Profit from the Core: Growth Strategy in an Era of Turbulence* (Boston: Bain & Company, Inc., 2001).

Index